Dear Michele

The 312 Best Things About Being a Stepmom

Love,

Rebekah,
and
Love matthew.

The 312 Best Things About Being a Stepmom

(For those days when you can only come up with one or two on your own)

by Cynthia L. Copeland

WORKMAN PUBLISHING • NEW YORK

Library of Congress Cataloging-in-Publication Data is
available.

Cover design by Paul Gamarello and Janet Parker
Interior design by Janet Parker

Workman books are available at special discount when
purchased in bulk for premiums and sales promotions as
well as for fund-raising or educational use. Special
editions or book excerpts also can be created to
specification. For details, contact the Special Sales
Director at the address below.

Workman Publishing Company, Inc.
708 Broadway
New York, NY 10003-9555

www.workman.com

Printed in the United States of America
First Printing March 2006
10 9 8 7 6 5 4 3 2 1

For every stepmother in search
of that elusive silver lining

Acknowledgments

Thanks, as always, to the wonderful
Margot Herrera, my editor, who inspires
and guides me, and to the other Workman
folks who contributed so much to this
book: Janet Parker and Paul Gamarello
for their creative design work, Joelle Herr
for production editorial, and the superb
Mari Kraske for publicity.

I would also like to express my gratitude
to the many women who spoke to me
about their stepmomming experiences.

Contents

INTRODUCTION: The Stepmom Forecast— *Cloudy with a Chance of Silver Linings* ..viii

CHAPTER ONE: Stepping Up as the Other Mother—*The Universal Aspects of Stepmotherhood* 1

CHAPTER TWO: Suddenly Stepmom—*From Single Gal to Married with Children* 54

CHAPTER THREE: Adding to the Flock— *Combining Kids for a Real-Life Brady Bunch* 102

CHAPTER FOUR: Nonstop Stepmom— *When Your Stepchildren Live with You Full-Time* 160

CHAPTER FIVE: Baby Steps— *Stepparenting Infants and Toddlers* 204

CHAPTER SIX: Next Steps—
The Middle Ages 240

CHAPTER SEVEN: Big Steps—
Life with Tweens and Teens 272

CHAPTER EIGHT: Giant Steps—*When Your
Little Steps Are Finally Grown* 326

CHAPTER NINE: Grown and Gone—*Becoming
a Stepmom When His Kids Are Adults* . . .354

CHAPTER TEN: In Step with Your Husband—
Making Your Marriage the Priority 382

CONCLUSION:
Silver Linings Found . . .418

The Stepmom Forecast

Cloudy with a Chance of Silver Linings

From the unexpected Mother's Day card to the sweet and sleepy good-night phone call from across town, the rewards of being a stepmother are many, though they often feel overshadowed by the monumental challenges of the job.

No wonder. With no clear expectations, no widely accepted job description or road map to follow, stepmothering can seem like a series of stutter steps and stabs in the dark. In the first years, it may bring more heartache than happiness, more frustration than fun. Studies have shown that of all of the members of a stepfamily, stepmothers suffer from the highest level of stress. And we often suffer silently in a culture where "real" mothers are revered and stepmothers are

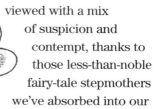

viewed with a mix of suspicion and contempt, thanks to those less-than-noble fairy-tale stepmothers we've absorbed into our collective psyche.

But even though I've waded through difficult times with all three of my stepsons, I have also been the recipient of unexpected hugs, heartwarming cards and letters, and thoughtful gestures. And part of a stepmother's job involves moving quickly past the rough patches—the hurtful acts and words—and lingering over the good moments. We learn to forgive and move on, for the sake of our marriages and our own sanity, and we try to give our stepkids—who are also treading through unknown territory—the benefit of the doubt.

When a stepmother-stepchild relationship works—and most eventually do—it is because both people have chosen to work at it. They begin with no shared history, no mutual understanding built on years of togetherness, no unconditional love. And despite that, they make a conscious decision to expend the effort to learn about and, eventually, to care about each other.

There will no doubt be plenty of dark moments, but it's worth it to focus on the bright side. Consider the blessings offered up in this book and look at it this way: The layers of storm clouds overhead and on the horizon also have the potential for plenty of silver linings.

Chapter One

Stepping Up as the Other Mother

The Universal Aspects of Stepmotherhood

Let's be honest. No one dreams of growing up and becoming a stepmother. But even though it wasn't part of your life plan, it can still be a very positive and enriching experience.

Many of the rewards that come with being a stepmom are universal. Whether you're combining "his" and "hers" kids or stepping solo into a ready-made family, whether you're coping with colic or curfews, stepmoms share many insights and uplifting experiences. Some are life-altering, others fleeting. Some are amusing and some are heartwarming. But all are part of stepmomming.

World's best ♥ step mom

1

Having children around reminds you to play.

Your stepkids will not demand that you read to them when they're in the bathroom.

As a stepparent, you worry less about what a child will become and enjoy what he is today.

It won't hurt your dad's feelings that none of your stepkids are named Homer Eugene Harrington III.

You learn what the term
"roll with the punches" really means.

You can spoil them a little.

Stepparenting fosters empathy. You'll feel a bond with other families that have two or three different last names on the mailbox.

A Day of Our Own

In 1997, September 16 was established as Stepfamily Day. To find other stepfamilies that might also be celebrating, check out the Stepfamily Association of America (SAA) Web site: www.saafamilies.org. If there is no SAA chapter in your area, the Web site offers tips on how to start your own support group.

"I found it so helpful and reassuring to talk regularly with a group of other stepmoms. We shared our concerns and offered advice to one another. And, I'll admit, sometimes we just vented. But it alleviated everyone's anxiety, I think, to realize that the problems we were having were not unique to us but were a normal part of becoming a stepfamily."

—Caroline, mother of one, stepmother of three

8

Y̶ou can tell your stepson
that you think it's *wonderful*
he wants to be a three-headed
dragon for Halloween without
worrying about how to make
the costume.

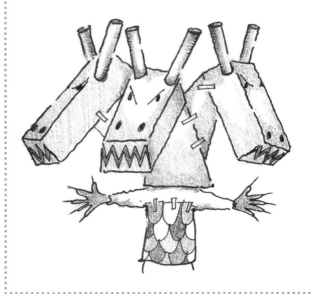

"My stepdaughter and I began bonding when we would take part of the weekend to do things for 'our' guy (her dad). We'd wash his car, match his socks, or make his favorite dinner. She was happy to be doing something for him, and it definitely helped to lessen any competition between us."

—Sophia,
stepmother of one

"The stepfamily's strength and vitality lie in its differentness. . . ."

—Karen Savage and Patricia Adams, authors, on why stepfamilies should not try to mimic biological families

"We must accept finite disappointment, but we must never lose infinite hope."

—Martin Luther King Jr.

9

You don't take their little quirks personally. (Hey, those aren't *your* genes rearing their kooky heads!)

10 The more intimate relationships we have in our lives, the richer we are.

11 Your stepson's hamster, "housebroken" bunny, and iguana all live at his mother's house.

"Recently, we hiked to the summit of a nearby mountain with four of our kids. As I followed them, I watched the kids swinging hands, singing, laughing, and playing tag and hide-and-go-seek along the trail. I hope that someday their feelings of loss and confusion fade, and our shared memories of Saturday badminton games and Sunday family dinners take their place."

—Helen, mother of three, stepmother of two

Fairy tales haven't set very high expectations for stepmothers, so you're bound to look good in comparison.

"Better to giggle with the children about being their Evil Stepmother than to have the unspoken notion that I really am evil constantly lurking in their minds."

—Bronwyn Lance Chester, newspaper columnist

Wicked Stepmother Pitfalls

Fairy-tale stepmothers get a pretty bad rap, but they do make some rather unfortunate errors. Let's try to learn from their mistakes.

- Don't insist on being the fairest in the land.

- If your stepdaughter begs to try on a glass slipper or wants a fancy new dress for the ball, be supportive. When she marries her prince, she'll remember that you were in her corner.

- Don't force your stepdaughter to sweep the fireplace or do the mending unless your kids are doing it, too. Treat everyone fairly.

- Never try to trick your stepchildren by offering them poisoned fruit when their dad isn't watching and sweet treats when he is. Kids aren't easily fooled.

- If you discover your stepdaughter cooking and cleaning for seven little men, let her be. She'll figure out soon enough that there's an easier way to get free room and board. Save the lecture and let life teach the lesson.

- Don't leave your stepchildren deep in the forest with only a bit of bread. That's just not going to play well after the fact, no matter how you tell it.

- Talking to your mirror is not all that productive. You're better off calling your mother.

17

"**T**wo myths must be shattered: that of the evil stepparent . . . and the myth of instant love, which places unrealistic demands on all members of the blended family. . . . Between the two opposing myths lies reality."

—Claire Berman, author

You don't have to match their
socks (at least not very
often). But you do get to
surprise your
stepdaughter with
the Hello Kitty
socks she fell in
love with at the
mall.

13

You're the backup Santa and
Easter Bunny: less pressure,
just as much fun.

14

15 There are more people who want to hold your hand.

16 As a stepmom, you often get bonus points for doing things they simply expect of their "real" parents.

17 You don't feel compelled to give them practical gifts like clothing for holidays and birthdays. You can give fun stuff like skateboards or scooters.

"Stepfamilies are normal. They've been around as long as tribal members raised the children of dead or disabled bioparents. They've probably been the majority family type, across centuries and cultures, until modern health care has greatly reduced the global human mortality rate this past century."

—Peter Gerlach, MSW, researcher and therapist

The Name Game

Most stepkids refer to their stepmom by her first name or a nickname. Some stepmoms go by a combination of Mom or Mama and a first name, like Mama Ruth, or by a Mom-soundalike such as Mimi or Mum. Others choose a nickname that reflects a bond between the stepchild and stepmother. If both love jelly beans, then J.B. might work. Some other options include Noni, Omi, or Ima, which have all come to mean "other mother." And there's always S'mom, short for Stepmom.

The important thing is that both stepmom and stepchild are comfortable with the name, and that neither feels it was forced upon him or her. Gailzilla or Smellen, for instance, would not be acceptable.

"**I** told my young stepson that he could call me whatever he was comfortable with. I was expecting 'Carrie' just because that's what he hears his dad call me, but he announced he would call me 'Care Bear' after one of his favorite stuffed animals!"

—Carrie, mother of two,
stepmother of one

"Most important is the recognition that stepparenting is different from primary parenting. It can be just as satisfying, it can be a reciprocally loving and caring relationship between parent and child, and it can provide some very good moments when it works, but it is different."

—Claire Berman, author

The Christmas tree will get decorated faster, and present-opening will last longer.

18

Tips for Making Holidays Merry

1. Be flexible. You don't need to celebrate a holiday on its official date. Why not celebrate Thanksgiving on Friday rather than Thursday? As kids grow up and marry, it's more likely that your alternative day of celebration won't conflict with the new in-laws.

2. Plan ahead. Talk with ex-spouses well in advance so that the children know what the plan will be and don't feel that it's their obligation to accommodate all the various adults.

3. Plan well. Rather than making several trips to visit relatives, invite everyone to your house for one meal.

4. Count your blessings. Focus on the advantages of being a stepfamily:

Maybe all the kids will be gone on Christmas Eve, giving you and your husband a special night together.

5. Focus on the fun. Don't get so bogged down with your to-do list that you lose sight of the joy a holiday brings.

6. Point out the advantages to the kids. You can validate a child's sadness around the holidays, but also point out the positives—more celebrations, a variety of traditions, and more siblings to rejoice with.

7. Prioritize. Decide what you value most about a given holiday and put it at the top of your list: If you can't bear to miss the *Messiah* sing-along, plan other activities around it.

"It is the quality of relation-ships, not the type of family, that makes a difference to the psychological well-being of children."

—Susan Gamache, MA, RCC, counselor and researcher

"That the birds of worry and care fly above your head, this you cannot change . . . but that they build nests in your hair, this you can prevent."

—Chinese proverb

19

The passage of time, which likely has not been something you have thought of fondly, now becomes a friend. As time passes, your family feels more like one.

20

Every child is an artist. Your stepkids will inspire you.

21 Now there are other little people who will call your mom "Grammy."

22 Everyone could use a few more homemade pot holders.

23 You learn to be flexible: Although you can't control the wind, you can adjust the sails.

" At a yard sale, my stepson bought a cute little figurine with a saying about grandmothers. I assumed it was for my husband's mother. But the next time my parents came to visit, he brought it out and gave it to my mother. She was very moved, and I thought it was such a sweet gesture on his part. "

—Valerie, mother of two,
stepmother of two

"Fulfilling the role of step-mother gives us a unique opportunity to create more love and open-heartedness in the world. It's easy . . . to love the children who come to life under our own hearts, but it's not always effortless to open our hearts to the children who come to us as part of our marriage package."

—Sue Patton Thoele, author

The initial adjustment period is a lot like labor pains—as your love for the child grows, the painful memories fade. **24**

You're not obsessed with whether they're "normal." **25**

Rather than being amused or annoyed, you feel a kinship with the women who lurk near the doorway of the men's restroom shouting, "Eric?! You okay in there?!" **26**

STEPMOTHERS AROUND THE WORLD

Here's what you might be called in another country:

France:
belle-mère

Italy:
matrigna

Norway:
stemor

Germany:
stiefmutter

Spain:
madrastra

Poland:
macocha

Netherlands:
stiefmoeder

Portugal:
madrasta

Serbia:
maćeha

"My relationship with my stepson's mother began to improve when we both signed up to be 'room mother' for his first-grade class. When the year started, it was a bit awkward, but eventually it contributed to a stronger relationship between us, which is so much better for Jamie. Things are not always perfect, but we consider her part of our family and she considers my kids and me part of hers."

—Jenn, mother of two,
stepmother of one

Setting a Good *Ex*-ample

When you married your husband, you also married his first family, including his ex-wife. Though she may not behave kindly or even rationally in your presence, you can only control you. So consider the suggestions below, and, no matter how his ex-wife responds, you can pat yourself on the back for having taken the high road.

1. Try to imagine how she feels as she is packing her child's suitcase every other Friday afternoon. Empathy dilutes anger.

2. Reassure her that you will honor her role as their mother and that you are not trying to replace her.

3. Don't be excessively affectionate with the kids in front of her.

4. Temper your enthusiasm to charge full-force into stepmotherhood. Take it slowly and give everyone—including his ex—time to adjust.

5. If you disagree in matters of child rearing, defer to her (unless the children are genuinely at risk).

6. When you see her, smile and say hello. She may ignore you, but then again, she may not.

7. Don't push her buttons. If she's a stickler for promptness, drop the kids off on time.

8. Establish limits and boundaries, but encourage communication between

your husband and his ex to discuss
matters involving the kids.

9. Consult her before you sign up for
room mom, soccer mom, or any other
"mom" position.

10. Accept the fact that the relationship between the two of you will
probably always be a challenging one.

" After all is said and done, outdoing your husband's ex-wife is an empty victory, because instead of concentrating on the positive aspects of your marital relationship you are concentrating on achieving a goal that makes another individual look deficient. At the same time, this allows the other person to have undue influence in your life. "

—Karen Savage and Patricia Adams, authors

27 You can be his biggest fan on the sidelines, but when it's your stepson's turn to host the rugby team for dinner, chances are pretty good that it won't fall on one of your nights.

28 Being a stepmom can be the best of both worlds: You get to spend time with the children, and you get to spend time alone with your husband when his kids are with their mom and yours are with their dad.

"My stepdaughter is a bit forgetful when it comes to putting her dirty clothes in the laundry room and picking up her bedroom. I really don't like to nag, so I left her a note reminding her of a few chores she needed to do, written in a light-hearted way and signed 'Your Wicked Stepmother.' When I got home from work, she had left the note in the kitchen with check marks by the chores she had done and had written 'UN' in before 'wicked.'"

—Stephanie, mother of two, stepmother of three

41

29

As a stepmom, you have lots of opportunities to earn points toward sainthood—or, if you're a Buddhist, a truly awesome reincarnation.

"God will not look you over for medals, degrees, or diplomas, but for scars."

—Elbert Hubbard, author

How to Become a Saint

You may think your role as a stepmother automatically qualifies you (and *I* would certainly back you on that one), but there are a few other things to be considered:

1. You must have been dead for at least five years, but it helps to have been dead for centuries. (This rule's a real bummer because sainthood is one of those things that would look pretty impressive on your résumé.)

2. There must be proof that you're in heaven, so your life should have been a model of holiness and heroic virtue. This means that getting up at 5:00 a.m. twice a week to take your stepdaughter to hockey practice wasn't for naught.

3. Once you pass hurdle No. 2, people who knew you will be interviewed and your personal writings gathered. (Note: Chuck that journal your therapist advised you to keep after your stepson invited a few of the guys from his "band" to move in with you—just, you know, until they could get a decent gig.)

4. Finally, you must have performed miracles that defy medical science. Bringing your son's hamster back to life after you stepped on it probably does not qualify, but convincing your stepdaughter to take chemistry rather than study hall probably does. (If you are a martyr, the miracle requirement can be waived. Something to consider.)

44

"My stepdaughter, who is one of the top gymnasts in the state, is always pushing herself to the limit. Sometimes she'll come to our house completely spent and exhausted. A few weeks ago, she was tearfully talking about the pressures she was feeling, and I was listening and suddenly she wrapped her arms around me. She didn't say a word. She just hugged me for a long time. I was sorry she was so stressed out, but the hug felt great."

—Barb, stepmother of two

"I feel good about my role as mediator between my stepson and his father. There are times when he is afraid to talk to his dad right away and he comes to me first. I am a safe adult who cares about him, but I don't have the degree of emotional investment that his biological parents do. Together we develop strategies so that he can share things with his dad without starting an argument."

—Rhonda, mother of two, stepmother of three

46

Comfort in Numbers

According to the Stepfamily Foundation, every day 1,300 new stepfamilies are formed. By 2010, the U.S. Census Bureau predicts that there will be more stepfamilies than traditional families (true biological families) or single-parent families.

30 Stepparenthood can't be rushed, so you can legitimately sit back, relax, smile, and just let it happen.

"Children require guidance and sympathy far more than instruction."

—Annie Sullivan,
Helen Keller's teacher

Empathy 101

Looking at Life Through the Eyes of Your Stepchildren

It's easier to forgive your step-children's unkind remarks or behavior when you imagine how the stepfamily experience must make them feel.

• Though you consciously decided to become a stepmother, they did not choose to become stepchildren.

• They may feel partly responsible for the divorce.

• They mourn the loss of their biological parents as a couple and sometimes wish that their original family was back together.

• They have less alone time with their

dad now that he has you in his life. Sometimes they feel less important to him.

- They feel like they are betraying their mom by forming a relationship with you.

- They are worried that you won't like them.

- Going back and forth between two houses is disorienting.

- They may question your commitment to them and to this new family.

- They hate being grilled by one parent about the other parent's household. They also hate being asked to lie to the other parent.

"Families that survive best seem to have two things going for them. One is being able to talk about emotions. . . . The other is providing both a sense of autonomy and a feeling of connectedness. In this regard, nuclear families could learn a lot from the adjustments stepparents and children have had to make, changes in protocol that, when successful, assure that everyone is both respected and loved."

—Madeline Drexler,
journalist and author

31 Because you haven't heard your stepson practice "Blue Note Rock" 87 times over the past four months, the band concert is a pleasant surprise.

★ **Celebrity Stepmom** *When Jada Pinkett Smith married husband Will, she became stepmom to his son Trey. She refers to Trey as her "bonus son," and says she is "looking for a picture for Trey and I to do together."*

"A counselor shared something with me that has made my life so much easier. She said that my job as a stepmother was to step back. Once I didn't feel like I had to solve everyone's problems and make everybody happy all the time, I could enjoy the good times and let the kids' father and mother manage the crises."

—Eliza, mother of two, stepmother of two

Chapter Two

Suddenly Stepmom

*From Single Gal to
Married with Children*

As you echo "for better, for worse" and prepare for the kiss that seals the deal, you catch a glimpse of the ring bearer—your true love's little boy— sticking his tongue out at you. Just for a moment, you wonder exactly how bad that "worse" might get. Is it possible that the man of your dreams comes with a 9-year-old nightmare?

Don't panic. Although many childless women view a marriage that includes stepchildren as a wonderful opportunity to experience parenthood, other women are overwhelmed and a bit frightened by the idea of an instant family. Stepchildren mean significant changes in lifestyle and a shift in priorities. But if you can relax, step back, and examine the proverbial big picture, you will recognize that the opportunity to inspire a growing person is an awesome one that will influence many generations to come. You may look back someday and rank your role in raising your husband's children as one of your greatest legacies.

And remember: The 9-year-old who stuck out his tongue at the wedding may well become the 16-year-old who offers to mow the lawn when your husband is traveling for business. Loving and nurturing a child is never a wasted effort.

32 You can play on the swings without looking ridiculous.

33 You have willing teachers to show you how to do cool yo-yo tricks, how to make a daisy chain, and how to spin a basketball on your index finger.

34 You didn't have to decide whether to name him after his grandfather, his rich uncle, or your favorite poet.

"When I married Dan, he had three children, and I had none. I had a lot of trouble understanding his relationship with his kids. Now that he and I have a 4-year-old, I finally get it. I understand the depth of attachment and emotion. Having a child of my own has made me a much better stepmother."

—Sarah, mother of one, stepmother of three

35 When you are forced to explain things to an inquisitive child, you come to understand them better yourself.

"Your first butterfly. Your first rainbow. Your first dinosaur. In sharing your childhood, I relived my own."

—Pam Brown, poet

You have a good excuse to
get a bigger house.

36

37 If you are thinking about having kids of your own, you don't have to wonder what kind of father your husband will be—whether he's the kind of dad who will run tirelessly beside a bike after the training wheels have come off or who will get up early to make pancakes for Saturday's breakfast. You're an eyewitness to his parenting.

Now you can get a horse— "for the kids."

Other Fun Things You Can Legitimately Get Now... "For the Kids"

a swimming pool

a trampoline

the Disney channel (and all the other channels that come with it)

39 You get to be a role model!

40 Sometimes you're privy to secrets your stepdaughter doesn't feel comfortable sharing with her parents.

"[Parenting] forces us to get to know ourselves better than we ever might have imagined we could—and in many new ways. . . . We'll discover talents we never dreamed we had. . . . As time goes on, we'll probably discover that we have more to give and can give more than we ever imagined. . . ."

—Fred Rogers

Stepmother Shower

One day you were childless, and the next day: Voilà! Instant stepchildren! In a culture chock-full of rites of passage and celebrations, women slip silently into stepmotherhood, unsupported and unnoticed. That's a shame, because rituals are important: They allow us to glean information about a new stage of life, say good-bye to an old life, and feel community support.

You can get a fellow stepmother off to a positive start by throwing her a shower before she becomes a stepmom, much like pregnant women are given baby showers. Guests can bring books on parenting and stepparenting, romantic gifts for the new couple, family games, photo albums—any token of her new life.

41

You will learn everything there is to know about fairies and unicorns, dinosaurs and dragons, princesses and ponies, pirates and knights, excavators and cement mixers.

If you rub the horn of a unicorn, your wish will come true!

To become a knight, you get hit with the flat part of the sword on your shoulder!

"My husband and I were not scheduled to have his son during the first week of school, but as soon as he got home on the first day, he called to tell us all about it. He wanted to tell me specifically about his art class, because I love to paint with water-colors. It was very sweet."

—Angie, stepmother of one

If you walk your stepchild to the bus stop now and then, you'll meet lots of other neighborhood moms you otherwise might not get to know.

42

You can brag about your stepkids' report cards without seeming like a show-off.

43

Now you have an excuse
to rent *101 Dalmatians*.

"**I** was having a bad day last week. I walked into the kitchen to make dinner and noticed a paper cup full of wildflowers on the counter. My younger stepdaughter had written a note that said, 'Hope you're feeling better.' And right then, I started feeling better."

—Kathleen, stepmother of two

45 You have help when you try to talk your husband out of wearing tube socks with Tevas.

46

You can make a significant contribution to the whole nature-versus-nurture debate by determining whether your inexplicable fear of the number 13 and obsession with flossing your teeth pass down to your stepchildren.

47

It will be easier for you to have an honest, productive conversation with your stepteens about mistakes you made at their ages.

"I was out of town on business a few months ago when my cell phone rang. It was my stepdaughter— she had asked her dad if it was all right to call me and ask how my trip was going. I was so touched!"

—Elyse, stepmother of two

Whereas most moms have to take whatever comes out, you get to "try before you buy." 48

You have the opportunity to view daily life through the eyes of a child: A nighttime power outage, for instance, is a thrilling adventure—not an inconvenience 49

And then the WOLF jumped out from behind a tree...

Mom Vocabulary 101

With instant motherhood comes mom-speak. Suddenly, you sound less like you and more like your own mom. You'll hear yourself saying traditional mom things, even things you vowed you'd never say. Here are a few momisms you're bound to let slip:

- I think your eyes are bigger than your stomach.

- Life isn't fair.

- Because I said so.

- It takes two to tango.

- I've had it up to *here*!

74

- Money doesn't grow on trees.

- The fresh air will do you good.

- I'm not talking just to hear the sound of my own voice!

- If you're too sick to go to school, you're too sick to _____ (fill in the blank).

- Feet off the table.

- The important thing is that you did your best.

- Be patient! I can't be in five places at once.

- I can't hear myself think!

- Two wrongs don't make a right.

- Take it or leave it.

50

Vacuuming under the sofa cushions is much more of an adventure now.

Latest Haul

barrette

65¢

Sponge Bob gummy

Lego body

Barbie shoe and comb

guitar pick even though no one plays guitar

Skittles

Unidentifiable object stepson found on playground

one-day old rubber band ball

Part of a McDonald's Happy Meal toy

Y ou learn all sorts of new things as a stepmom, like what it costs to replace a brand-new clarinet that was left at the bus stop and how much two speeding tickets will add to a 17-year-old boy's car insurance.

51

Y ou have built-in time alone or time with friends when your husband is busy with his kids.

52

"I had always wanted children, but for a variety of reasons, it didn't happen. When I finally met the man of my dreams and got married, I was in my late 40s. Being able to share in the lives of my stepchildren has been a blessing. It has helped me get over a lot of the sadness I've felt in not having my own biological children."

—Debbie, stepmother of three

Y ou expand your capabilities
    for patience, tolerance, and
compromise.

53

"W hen one door of happiness
    closes, another opens;
but often we look so long at the
closed door that we do not see
the one which has been opened
for us."

—Helen Keller

54 You will get enough school papers to properly cover the front of the refrigerator, but not so many that you will be forced to devote half of your attic space to school memory boxes.

55 You may be the only one in your office who knows that Picachu is not a foreign leader and that Strawberry Shortcake is not just a dessert.

Being intimately—if sporadically—involved in your teenage stepkids' love dramas reminds you how nice it is to be older and married.

"He told Sarah he liked ME but then Kate saw him at STEPHANIE'S locker and they were WHISPERING and then he didn't say hi to me at lunch and he sat with ALYSSA on the bus...."

57 Your fifth-grade stepson will probably go to his father for help with his math homework, so the fact that you have no clue what a Venn diagram is will stay your little secret.

58 You may catch that "bug" that's been going around your stepdaughter's class, but you'll also find that her energy and enthusiasm are contagious.

Celebrity Stepmom *In her memoir,* Leap of Faith, *Queen Noor of Jordan describes how, in marrying King Hussein, she became stepmother to his eight children. Although there were times when she felt "completely helpless, responsible, and very much alone, . . . as in most families, patience and faith were rewarded over the following years. . . . We shared [our children's] disappointments and delights, and rejoiced in their marriages and children. These were some of the happiest and most hopeful times of my life."*

"**M**y stepdaughter had to write an essay for school about the person she most admired. She wrote about me and said that she loved the way I am so happy to see her when she comes to visit. She'll never know that there were times when the smile was forced, but it was well worth it!"

—Vicky, stepmother of three

84

J ust when you thought that maybe you were all done with those "growth" and "character building" experiences, here's a biggie!

59

Y ou will learn all of the ways broccoli can be hidden on or around a dinner plate.

60

I f you ever decide to have kids of your own, you've had practice.

61

The Stepmother Litmus Test

Your success as a stepmother is assured if:

1. Between 5:30 a.m. (when your stepdaughter realizes that she "totally spaced" on her social studies project) and 8:10 a.m. (when the bus comes), you can help her whip together a scale model of the White House using an egg carton, four toilet paper tubes, a shoe box, and two coffee cans.

2. You can make one dinner that meets with the approval of all four stepchildren (as well as your husband): the kid who will not allow anything on his plate that has bones in it and will not eat cheese; the kid who will only eat cheese (but it has to be Muenster because it sounds like "monster"); the kid who won't eat anything green and must eat with chopsticks; the kid who will chew only twice before swallowing; and the husband who wants everything to taste deep-fried but have no cholesterol.

3. You are not thrown by a child's odd little quirks, including, but not limited to, being afraid of balloons or any item that might at some point "pop," sleeping under the bed rather than on top of it, wanting his food served to him on the floor so he can eat like a puppy, and preferring to cuddle with last year's phone book rather than the stuffed dog you got him for his birthday.

62

Your stepdaughter will stop by in her prom dress so you can take pictures, but you didn't have to go through the three weeks of dress selection, two hours of hair and makeup, and three meltdowns because of a broken nail, a pimple, and a lost earring.

"As a childless person, I was very nervous about marrying a man with two teenagers. But I've found that there have been many more positives than negatives. I'd always considered myself relatively savvy, but I didn't realize how out of touch I'd become with popular music, fashion, and pop culture in general. It's kind of fun to be the only one in my office who knows who Usher is."

—Lisa, stepmother of two

63   You are forced to leave your dynamic, take-charge professional personality at the office because you can't rush a stepfamily.

" **A**lways try to be a little kinder than is necessary."

—James Barrie, playwright and novelist

"**I**'ve had four stepmothers . . . and have been a stepmother myself. The secret, in a word, is: relax. Do your job; lower your expectations; do not be needy (you're the grown-up, after all); be empathetic and compassionate; say little, be patient."

—Kathleen Parker, columnist

64 Parenting in any form is a humbling experience, and a little humility is good for all of us.

65 People can't figure out how old you are by the ages of your stepchildren—why, you could have been ten when the oldest was born. . . .

66 You'll learn the fine art of cutting something *exactly* in half.

Learning to negotiate with a 5-year-old will help when you need to deal with your immature yet wily boss.

Okay... how about THIS? You can stay up one half hour later on Friday night, but you have to be playing quietly in your room and then you can't wake anyone up on Saturday morning before 8:00. Deal?

"Is it not possible that through parenting some people cultivate characteristics that enhance the way they perform at work? That many qualities developed through parenting may, in some instances and in certain ways, contribute to career development?"

—Elin Schoen, author and journalist

Now you can use those same excuses the other mothers in your office do: "I'll have to leave the meeting a little early to see my stepson's soccer game" or "I can't come in on Saturday because my stepdaughter is having a dance recital."

69 You now understand the contentment and serenity parents experience when they watch their children sleep.

70 Now you have someone to pass along your teacup collection to (and your secret recipes and grandmother's charm bracelet).

71

If the kids are acting up in public and people begin to look accusingly at you, you can say, "Now you'd better behave, or I'm going to tell your mother!" thus absolving yourself of some responsibility.

72

You suddenly feel inspired to call and thank your own parents for raising you.

73

Kids always sense when you need a hug.

"**P**ace yourself . . . an elephant can be swallowed, one bite at a time."

—**Proverb**

"**E**very once in a while, my stepson will slip up and call me 'Mom' rather than Nancy. When that happens, I realize how far we've come in a couple of years."

—**Nancy, stepmother of one**

74

Having three or four "parents" increases the odds that someone will have an extra vehicle when he turns sixteen, be willing to host his graduation party, or pitch in with the wedding when she finds the man of her dreams.

75

By the time you realize that family life is less like the Osmonds and more like the Osbournes, you're already committed and starting to bond with your very own "Kelly."

76 You can teach him how to speak in pig latin toward the end of your weekend, knowing that the novelty will have worn off before the next visit.

77 No one at the office will be able to stump you with the latest knock-knock joke.

78 You have to make up stories —bedtime and otherwise— on the fly, allowing you to discover latent storytelling talents.

You begin to realize that, at the end of the day, helping to build people is a lot more satisfying than helping to build a bridge or build up a law practice.

79

"Nothing you do for children is ever wasted."

—Garrison Keillor,
author and radio show host

Chapter Three

Adding to the Flock

Combining Kids for a Real-Life Brady Bunch

Carol Brady made it look easy, but c'mon—not one episode of *The Brady Bunch* required her to drive two children and four friends to a travel soccer game while simultaneously taking a group of Boy Scouts white-water rafting *and* making four dozen cupcakes for a cheerleading bake sale. And let's not forget that she had Alice as a backup and no ex-spouses lurking about.

Combining two families—daunting though it may seem at first—offers an opportunity for a fresh start. There is no such thing as a "typical" stepfamily, so you get to make up your own rules as you go along!

Don't be disappointed if the children need some time to connect with one another and with you. The reality is that it may take years—possibly five or six years—for everyone to settle in and accept the new family dynamic. Relax, be patient, and celebrate the positive milestones. You may not believe it today (as you listen to them fighting over the PlayStation 2 controls), but years from now, your son and stepson will likely seek each other out, even if they live far from one another. And, years from now your daughter and stepdaughter may spend hours on the phone, even though they can't exchange two civil words today. Just wait.

80 You get more Mother's Day cards without having to add to your collection of stretch marks and varicose veins.

81 Your stepkids haven't heard all of your "when I was a kid" stories yet.

Combining children might mean that your only daughter now has sisters who will provide support and friendship throughout her adult life.

83 Your children cannot get away with complaining to you that there's no one to play with.

84 There is more to brag about in the holiday letter.

"Govern a family as you would cook a small fish—very gently."

—Chinese proverb

"Well, since the goat marionettes were – as you kids put it – lame-o, let's try a little singing ... Anyone know 'Edelweiss'?"

More kids gets you closer to that von Trapp family fantasy you've had since 8th grade.

85

"When we're all together at the dinner table and I hear one of the kids start a sentence with 'Remember when we . . . ' it just warms my heart. I realize that in two years we've already created some wonderful shared memories."

—Beth, mother of two, stepmother of two

Your son, who always hated being "the middle child," now gets to be the "second oldest." 86

You can buy that value-priced 24-pack of Popsicles with the confidence that they will all disappear before succumbing to freezer burn. 87

Family council now has enough people for a house *and* a senate. 88

" A strong, stable stepfamily is as capable of nurturing healthy development as a nuclear family. It can imbue values, affirm limits and boundaries, and provide a structure in which rules for living a moral and productive life are made, transmitted, tested, rebelled against, and ultimately affirmed."

—Dr. James H. Bray and John Kelly,
authors and researchers

You Know You're Really Bonded as a Family When . . .

- Your stepdaughter will spit her old gum into your hand.

- Everyone has a special place at the table.

- Your son gives his stepbrother bunny ears in a photo.

- The kids do a better job Christmas shopping for each other than you do.

- The kids are on each other's IM lists.

- Your teenage stepson remembers to rent a G-rated movie so his little stepbrother can watch too.

- The kids have weird nicknames for the various dinners you make that only they understand.

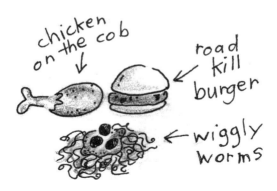

chicken on the cob ↓

road kill burger

← wiggly worms

- Your daughter refuses to speak to the girl in her homeroom who dumped her stepbrother.

- You can anticipate each other's adjectives in Mad Libs.

- The kids know each other's after-school schedules.

- Your stepdaughter asks you to make your famous banana bread for her Girl Scout bake sale.

- You automatically include your step-kids when someone asks how many kids you have.

- You remember to buy lemon yogurt before your stepson comes for a visit because that's his favorite.

- You agree on what constitutes a bad word.

- You miss them when they're not around.

"We had a lot of fun recording a new outgoing phone message after my husband and I got married. We let all of the kids participate, and I think it was the first tiny step toward feeling like a family."

—Michelle, mother of three,
stepmother of three

You get a lot of mileage out of
your parenting books.

89

90 Increasing your flock makes it more likely there'll be someone willing to push you around in your wheelchair when you're 91.

91 Based on tips from older siblings, the younger kids will know which teachers give pizza parties for good work and which ones pile on the weekend homework.

"I didn't think a lot about my parenting style before I had stepkids. I just did what I needed to do—I didn't analyze it. Stepparenting has forced me to examine my strengths and weaknesses as a parent and stepparent. It's made me parent more thoughtfully, more deliberately. I know I'm doing a better job because of that."

—Rosa, mother of three, stepmother of two

92 There will be more (and more competitive) Easter egg hunters, which means that it's less likely you'll find rotten eggs moldering in the woodpile come July.

93 More kids means more soccer goals, 4-H ribbons, and spelling bee victories to celebrate.

When it comes to teaching you how to do an attachment on the computer, your stepkids have more patience with you.

"You mean I hit <u>this</u> button?"
"No, hit the one next to it."
"This one?"
"No, the one <u>next</u> to it."
"Like this?"

"We must return optimism to our parenting. To focus on the joys, not the hassles; the love, not the disappointments; the common sense, not the complexities."

—Fred G. Gosman, author

"The bond that links your true family is not one of blood, but of respect and joy in each other's life."

—Richard Bach, author

You always thought you would have made a good team manager when you were in high school, and now you get a chance to see if you were right.

95

Your teenage stepson is always willing to take your 6-year-old son to the men's room when he needs to go (just when you were starting to get strange looks when you took him into the women's restroom with you).

96

Phases of a Stepfamily

A Four- to Seven-Year Plan

1. "The Sound of Music" or "Brady Bunch" Phase: Initially, you are in the fantasy stage in which naiveté and idealism reign. Hopes are high. You imagine you will all love each other totally and immediately.

2. The "Reality Check" Phase: Faced with the reality that your stepchildren may not accept you, your husband may not support you, and your family is anything but tranquil and loving, you feel upset and confused. You wonder what you've gotten yourself into.

3. The "Crazy, Hazy Days" Phase: You start to identify and articulate some of the specific issues that are bothering you and try to problem-solve. You are struggling as a family, and you begin to wonder whether the marriage will last. Conflict and chaos rule.

4. The "Coming Together" Phase: The family begins to listen and respond to the concerns of each person. Expectations become more realistic. Compromises are made; hurt feelings begin to mend; family members are learning to accept and tolerate one another.

5. The "Commitment" Phase: Members of the stepfamily form satisfying bonds with one another—stepparents with stepchildren and stepparents with each other—solidifying the marriage and stabilizing the family. The stepfamily becomes an accepted part of everyone's life.

97 More kids in your life means more people you can influence politically—Free Tibet!

98 Because they're not at your house all the time, stepkids consider walking the dog a novelty.

"When my daughter was born, I stopped working in an office to stay home and become a day-care provider. I offered to take care of my 4-year-old stepson, but his mother refused. A year or so later, she took me up on my offer. I think she knows that I love him like my own and I would take better care of him than someone outside the family. Ironically, she has even taken care of *my* children when I've had an emergency!"

—Diane, mother of one, stepmother of one

"When everyone starts saying 'we' instead of 'I.' And when everyone acknowledges, 'Wow, wasn't it awful? But we made it.'"

—Perdita Kirkness Norwood, author, on the signals that a stepfamily is undergoing positive change

"Too often we give children answers to remember rather than problems to solve."

—Roger Lewin, journalist and author

Marrying a man with older kids means having baby-sitters for your younger ones.

99

Marrying a man with younger kids means your kids have a great excuse to play with Legos and Playmobil again.

100

Wise Words
from Way Back

These age-old proverbs have stood the test of time. Do they ring true in your new expanded family?

- The more, the merrier.
- There's never a dull moment.
- Laughter is the best medicine.
- Time cures all things.
- Many hands make light work.
- Patience is a virtue.
- Love conquers all.
- United we stand, divided we fall.
- A woman's work is never done.
- No pain, no gain.
- After a storm comes a calm.

"As an only child, my daughter was always center stage. With two new (very active) stepbrothers participating in her birthday this year, I worried that she might feel lost in the shuffle. How wrong I was! The boys made her feel so special! It was much more fun having a bigger group. There will be ups and downs as we work toward becoming a family, but 'ups' like that will help us ride out the 'downs.'"

—Gina, mother of one, stepmother of two

101 You really get your money's worth out of your Internet connection, unlimited local calling plan, and cable TV.

102 With another hellion in the family, your son can relinquish his long-held title as the family mischief-maker.

"By their very nature, children have much to teach us. . . . For example, children often act as great models of acceptance and hospitality by embracing each other as siblings long before we adults are able to conceive of everyone as part of a cohesive whole."

—Sue Patton Thoele, author

Stepsibling Rivalry

*How to Keep Things
on an Even Keel*

- Trust the kids to work out most sibling issues among themselves.

- Resist your natural tendency to jump in and defend your own children; it will lead to greater problems down the road. Try to treat each child fairly so resentment doesn't build.

- If you have issues with any of your stepchildren, don't share them with your biological children. They will want to protect you, and that will affect their relationships with their stepsiblings.

- Praise the special qualities of each child to lessen the competition among them and make each one feel appreciated and loved.

- If possible, move to a new house when you combine families so that no one feels invaded and no one feels he's trespassing.

"There will always be some curveballs in your life. Teach your children to thrive in that adversity."

—Jeanne Moutoussamy–Ashe, photographer and wife of the late Arthur Ashe

"**O**ur best family times were vacations. The six kids really bonded with one another—there were no friends to compete for their time and no driving the kids all over town for activities. It was just the family, relaxing together and laughing together."

—Erica, mother of two, stepmother of four

Eventually, you'll have more grandkids!

103

When older relatives come to visit, your kids may get a break as Great-Aunt Betty focuses her mushy attention on the "new" kids.

104

"When the kids were younger, my husband and I took turns taking each child out for a special night once a month. The child could choose where to go and what to do. We didn't distinguish between kids and stepkids, which helped us feel closer."

—Sadie, mother of three, stepmother of two

Celebrity Stepchild *Growing up, Tom Hanks had two stepmothers and three stepfathers, and is one of 11 stepchildren. He claims he was at times referred to as Number 8.*

105 You might find that, by some odd twist of fate, you have a stepchild who "inherited" your passion for sailing, Parcheesi, or cake decorating.

106 Your children and stepchildren have more caring adults who'll be willing to help with an English essay, lend a hand setting up an electric train set, or teach them to golf.

107 Your stepchildren haven't had time to develop a dislike for your personal quirks, like the way you talk to yourself and pick the pretzels out of the snack mix.

" It's not going to work out overnight, but with time, kids will get the rich rewards of two families."

—Susan Shapiro Barash, author

" To overcome difficulties is to experience the full delight of existence."

—Arthur Schopenhauer, philosopher

There's more likely to be someone nearby who can give your daughter a push on the swing.

108

When your stepkids make a fuss over your chocolate zucchini cake, your own kids suddenly appreciate it a little more.

109

141

110 One-on-one time with each child is more valued and appreciated. No one takes it for granted.

111 The basement room will finally get finished because now you *really* need the extra space.

"The secret of health for both mind and body is not to mourn for the past, worry about the future, or anticipate troubles, but to live in the present moment wisely and earnestly."

—Buddha

7 Reasons Why Real-Life "Brady Bunch" Families Are Nothing Like the TV Sitcom

1. Real stepfamily problems can't be neatly resolved in 22 minutes.

2. Stepmoms who drink as much coffee as Carol aren't nearly as serene.

3. Three girls can not happily share a bedroom.

4. Three boys can happily share a bedroom, but it will be an absolute mess.

5. Three girls and three boys can never, ever share one bathroom—that doesn't even have a toilet!

6. In real life, doctors won't make house calls, even if all six of your children have the measles.

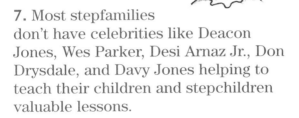

7. Most stepfamilies don't have celebrities like Deacon Jones, Wes Parker, Desi Arnaz Jr., Don Drysdale, and Davy Jones helping to teach their children and stepchildren valuable lessons.

But idealistic as it was, *The Brady Bunch* introduced the concept of a happy blended family to children of the '70s, minimizing the stigma associated with being part of a stepfamily. For that, we can all be thankful.

"**I** was nervous about combining families for a seven-child total, but I shouldn't have been. In a big family, you tend to let a lot of little things go and just deal with the larger issues, which is probably better for kids anyway. We just take a head count at dinner and if all seven are there, it was a good day!"

—Brenda, mother of four, stepmother of three

Y ou have reinforcements in the war on your son's algebra homework.

112

Y our family traditions multiply: Your kids are used to playing Pictionary on Friday nights and your stepkids are used to making pizza from scratch, so now you do both!

113

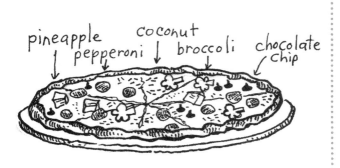

pineapple pepperoni coconut broccoli chocolate chip

114 There's no need to ship those hand-me-downs to the kids' cousins.

115 There are so many dirty clothes in the hamper that you can do a full load of just "reds"—why, you can probably do a full load of just "reddish-purples!"

116 The kids aren't all competing for one person's attention: There are lots of parents to go around.

"The first time my husband and I had to leave a note for both sets of kids, I scribbled the message and then was left wondering how to sign it. Not Mom and Dad. Not our first names. Finally, I just drew a little cartoon of the two of us. It turned out to be quite a hit! The kids thought it was a riot, so that has become our 'signature'!"

—Trish, mother of two,
stepmother of two

117 There are enough science fair projects and dioramas on the horizon to make it worthwhile to save toilet paper tubes, coffee cans, and shoe boxes.

"Family jokes, though rightly cursed by strangers, are the bond that keeps most families alive."

—Stella Benson, author

The trip to Sam's Club is finally worth the gas money.

151

Celebrity Stepmom *Teresa Heinz Kerry, wife of politician John Kerry and stepmother to his daughters Alex and Vanessa, commented that although there were conflicts when the families initially merged, as time goes by they continue to grow closer. "Like everything else," she said, "you go forward two steps, you go backward one."*

"...And then you know what Jacob did? He took a huge bite of clay because Mack DARED him to. And THEN you know what Jacob did? He ate a rubber band because Josh dared him to..."

"...And Susannah skinned her knee on the playground and I got to walk her to the nurse. And there were two first graders in there who were THROWING UP. And Susannah got a flower bandaid AND a flower sticker..."

You may still be the one doing the dishes, but there'll be more people to talk to while you do them.

119

"When school started, my 8-year-old stepson asked me if I would be the room mother for his class! It made sense because his mom works full-time and I am at home right now with my daughter, who is a baby. But I was so flattered that he wanted me!"

—Kim, mother of one,
stepmother of two

Stepfamily Bonding Movies

Be sure to rent these movies on family movie nights to give your kids and stepkids some good ideas:

The Sound of Music. The seven von Trapp children come to love their kind and spirited future stepmother Maria (Julie Andrews) despite some initial missteps. Will ring especially authentic if you were ever a nun, if you live in Austria, or if you can operate marionettes.

Yours, Mine, and Ours. The original comedy, based on a real-life couple, features Lucille Ball and

Henry Fonda as a widow and widower who marry and combine 18 (!) children into one family. In comparison, your gang will look paltry. A recent remake stars Dennis Quaid and Rene Russo.

With Six You Get Eggroll. In this 1968 comedy, Abby McClure (Doris Day) and Jake Iverson (Brian Keith) marry, combining her three sons and his teenage daughter. At first, the kids fight, but (get ready for the surprise ending) they gradually get to like each other as their parents work out a few kinks of their own.

The Brady Bunch Movie. Based on the popular 1970s TV show, this movie, comforting and nostalgic, is not a bad little comedy. It doesn't take itself too seriously, and you won't either.

. . . And Movies to Miss

The Parent Trap. Twins who were separated when they were babies are unknowingly sent to the same summer camp. There they scheme to reunite their parents, eliminating a potential evil stepmother in the process. Booooooo. . . .

Cinderella. Featuring the quintessential evil stepmother, this movie has poisoned generations of young minds. Double boooooo. . . .

"Things that you take for granted as a mother mean so much as a stepmother. The other day my 7-year-old stepdaughter searched me out to ask me if I would play with her. Of course my own kids ask that all the time, but she never had, so it really meant a lot to me."

—Eileen, mother of two,
stepmother of one

Having to share the bathroom, computer, and snack cupboard with extra people will make it easier for your kids to adjust to college dorm life.

120

By adding a few more participants to Friday game nights, there's a chance that you won't always get creamed in Scrabble.

121

Chapter Four

Nonstop Stepmom

*When Your Stepchildren
Live with You Full-Time*

Although most stepmothers are part-timers, some women are responsible for the full-time care of their stepchildren. These moms are often regarded as saint-like, admired for having "rescued" children whose biological mother either died or abandoned them. Though this societal reaction is preferable to disdain, it has its share of drawbacks. As one full-time stepmom said, "I'm not perfect. I don't want anyone to expect that kind of behavior from me. I get angry sometimes; I yell sometimes; I'm not always nice; and I don't want to feel guilty about that."

Many full-time stepmoms also feel pressured by the thought that there's little margin for error.

"These kids have already been through so much,"
one mom said, "that you just feel as if you can't
let them have a bad week. You have to fix it for
them somehow."

But there are special blessings. Most
stepmoms who've been at it for a number of
years admit that they stopped thinking "step"
long ago. "We're just a family," one woman said,
"and he's just my son."

122 Their friends always know where to call them.

123 Everyone will be with you on Mother's Day.

124 You really miss them when they're away at camp and can't wait for them to come back.

"I still have the first Mother's Day card my stepdaughter ever made for me. Her arrival earlier in the year had been a surprise to everyone, and the adjustment period was tough. So the fact that she spent so much time making a lovely card meant a great deal to me."

—Joyce, mother of two, stepmother of one

163

125 You'll be able to make sure they take their vitamins every day.

126 Your stepson doesn't spend the weekend pining for the PlayStation 2 and the pool table that are at his mom's.

"Come on, Ben! Don't you want to shoot some hoops? How about chess? Or cards? Do you want to help me work on the boat...?"

PS2... POOL TABLE

127 You and your husband don't have to pay child support—heck, you may even get some!

"Because my stepchildren live with us, we go to church every Sunday as a family—and I never have to worry that they might not have dress clothes with them! I feel like a mother duck when we walk into the sanctuary, with eight children following behind me. We fill an entire pew all by ourselves."

—Pam, mother of five,
stepmother of three

" A stepfamily can be a happy place to nurture adults and children alike and becomes much more like a biological family than single-parenting. "

—Kevin Ricker, MA, former president of the Stepfamily Association of America

You know their friends well enough to know which ones are likely to help them with algebra homework and which ones are likely to try to talk them into jumping off of the shed roof with a garbage bag as a parachute.

Will try to talk stepson into spending his allowance on a ferret

will stick old gum on top of TV

will help with science project

will eat last granola bar and put empty box back in pantry

The Kids' Friends

129 Because they're with you all the time, there is a greater chance that you'll be nearby when they feel like they really need someone to talk to.

130 You establish family traditions more quickly than part-time stepfamilies. Everyone knows that Friday nights mean take-out Chinese food and charades.

"Every Friday night a child gets to choose what we will have for dinner. Of course with younger kids, there's always the risk that you will have ice cream sundaes for dinner, which we've had!"

—Marie, mother of two, stepmother of three

"**T**hree years after she moved in with us, my stepdaughter called me 'Mom.' It touched me, but more than that, I felt a tremendous sense of achievement."

—Karen, stepmother of one

Your stepson will wear his "dad's house" snowsuit more than once before he outgrows it.

131

Your husband doesn't give them free rein out of the fear that they won't want to come back and visit.

132

171

8 Qualities of a Successful Stepmother

1. Humor: You can always see the humor in a given situation, which helps you—and those around you—cope.

2. Flexibility: With more people in your circle, plans are constantly changing. You're able to go with the flow.

3. Appreciation: You can appreciate the diverse, positive traits that everyone brings to the family and see your family for its blessings.

4. Sensitivity: You try hard to understand how each family member is feeling.

5. Perspective: You don't panic when the challenges seem overwhelming, but take comfort in the fact that things will get better and easier as time passes.

6. Kindness: You are loving and forgiving.

7. Inspiring: Though you won't replace their biological mom, you can be a positive role model and provide guidance.

8. Dedication: You let the children know that you will always be there for them. And you look for reasons to stay together rather than for a way out.

"I sensed some resentment from my teenage stepdaughters when I married their dad and moved in. (Their mom had moved overseas with another man.) I decided that my role should be more that of a big sister than a mother. I convinced their dad to relax his strict rules about their clothes, took them shopping, and offered to drive them places to make sure we had plenty of time for chatting. It's paid off. Years later, we're very close."

—Debbie, stepmother of two

The kids don't have to remember two sets of house rules.

133

134 You get all the notices he brings home from school, so you're never surprised by a science fair or winter concert.

135 No one has to live out of a suitcase for the weekend.

136 The kids are there to witness all of your marital spats, but also to witness the resolutions.

"My husband raised his own three by himself for several years. While that made their relationship very tight, which can be hard for me, it also made him a very hands-on parent who understands what my life is like now that I'm home with his kids and mine. He would be the last person to come home from work and say, 'So what did you do all day?'"

—Laura, mother of two, stepmother of three

137 When your own kids are with their dad, you have time to bond with your stepchildren without worrying about hurt feelings or jealousy.

138 You're comfortable enough around them to remind them to empty the dishwasher.

"When you get into a tight place and everything goes against you, till it seems you could not hold on a minute longer, never give up then, for that is just the place and time that the tide will turn."

—Harriet Beecher Stowe

Address the Stress

Did that giant step into stepmother-hood stress you out a bit? For a quick fix, just plunk yourself down in the midst of the chaos and embark on 10 minutes of breathing meditation:

Step 1. Sit in the traditional cross-legged meditation posture, keeping your back straight.

Step 2. With eyes partly closed, turn your complete attention to your breathing. Breathe naturally, through your nose, and concentrate on your breathing to the exclusion of everything else in the room, including your stepson who is putting toilet paper–tube rollers in your hair.

Step 3. Stay focused on your breathing. Resist the temptation to be distracted by other thoughts, and allow your mind to become still and clear.

Step 4. As other thoughts fade, you will feel a sense of inner peace and relaxation. You will be refreshed. And, thanks to your stepson, you will have a new hairdo.

139

You'll be up-to-date on all of the little things about your stepdaughter's life—like whether she still has a thing for the kid who sits behind her in French class, known as "Pierre," whether the PE unit on Ultimate Frisbee is finally over, whether Paige and Maggie are still mad at her.

"Biology is the least of what makes someone a mother."

—Oprah Winfrey

"You are trying to make a family out of chaos and heartbreak. All you can do is make everyone feel welcome and be incredibly kind."

—Louisa, mother of one, stepmother of two

"When my stepdaughter was about four, I was adding a quilt to her bed one chilly night, and she looked up at me and said, 'You feel like my mom.' I practically cried."

—Carly, mother of one, stepmother of one

"It stretches us all. We decided to become a family, and now each one of us has to ask, 'How am I going to love this person? How will I make these relationships work?'"

—Kim, mother of two, stepmother of four

When the pediatrician asks how long your step-daughter has had a cough and a fever, you'll know the answer.

140

If you get your stepson a puppy, he will actually be around to take care of it.

141

142 You can go skiing spontaneously because all the ski equipment is in your garage.

143 Everyone understands your family language, like what "poompsie" means.

Did someone do a prooky pie? I think so... "

They might even call you "Mommy."

144

"I've only been married to their dad for a year, so my stepkids don't call me 'Mom.' But they will say, 'I have to ask my mom about that.' It feels great."

—Erin, mother of three, stepmother of two

"She was the best thing that ever happened to me when I was a kid. She treated me like her own."

—Clark Gable on his stepmother, Jennie Dunlap Gable

"Five years after his mom died (and three years after I married his dad), my stepson introduced me to a new friend as his mother. I had always felt like his mother, but it was wonderful to know that he felt like my son."

—Jessie, stepmother of one

Chores can be evenly divided among all the kids, eliminating the suspicion that your stepson signs up for "Tuesday-putting-the-trash-out-duty" because he is never at your house on Tuesdays.

145

Every holiday is yours.

146

"One of the biggest challenges is finding the energy to parent a lot of kids, all the time. My three visit their dad regularly, but my stepchildren are here full-time, so I never have any built-in 'me' time. It's forced me to arrange time for activities that fulfill me. I run marathons, swim, and take guitar lessons. I think having to verbalize my needs and then act on them was a good lesson in putting myself near the top of my to-do list."

—Kristy, mother of three, stepmother of three

Stepmom Rights

Successful stepmothers gently but
firmly enforce their rights within
the family, knowing that allowing
themselves to be mistreated benefits
no one. Though as a stepmom you
need to be flexible and compassionate,
be aware that:

1. You deserve to be treated with respect
by every member of the family.

2. Your marriage deserves to be a top
priority.

3. You deserve to live in a home where
chores and responsibilities are shared
among all members of the family.

4. You deserve a voice in all family plans
and decisions that will involve or affect
you.

5. You deserve to live in a home where household rules are established and then enforced by both adults.

6. You deserve private space and time.

" As stepmoms, we should remember that in order to be walked on, we have to be lying down. It's our choice. "

—Dorothy, mother of two, stepmother of three

Their teachers treat you as first-string,
not a benchwarmer.

147

148 You don't need to run out and buy seconds of the things he has at his mom's that he always forgets to pack.

149 They can't escape being grounded by going to the other house.

150 Helping the kids deal with the departure of a biological mother can be easier than dealing with the actual mom.

"I tried to keep their memories of their mother alive. I wouldn't want to be forgotten by my children! The first thing I did when I moved into the house was take all the photos of her that had been tucked into a drawer and display them again."

—Diane, mother of three, stepmother of two

151 Full-time stepmothers are more accepted and appreciated in our society. Think Maria von Trapp and Carol Brady.

152 You can tuck everyone in at night and go to sleep knowing that they are all safe.

"My husband's first wife, who passed away several years ago, had a wonderful extended family. It didn't happen right away, but they now include my children from my first marriage in invitations for the kids to visit for a week or two without us. My kids love all of the new aunts, uncles, and cousins."

—Julia, mother of two, stepmother of three

A Stepfamily by Any Other Name

For those who don't like the term "stepfamily," here are some alternatives that other families have chosen:

- blended family

- extended family

- reconstituted family

- family of choice

- made-up family

- enlarged family

- bi-nuclear family

"I became a full-time stepmom when my husband's ex-wife moved across the country with a new boyfriend and severed all ties with her kids. Initially, I was resentful that I was left cleaning up the mess she left behind—the kids were confused and upset and acted out terribly. But I realized, after suffering the loss that they did, I had to be there for them one hundred percent. Two years later, we're doing better than before she left."

—Nina, mother of one, stepmother of three

"My husband had put his children in boarding school after their mother died because he thought that was best for them. I realized right away that they were miserable living at school. I suppose it would have made things easy on me to keep them there, but I just couldn't do it. I insisted that they come back home and I would care for them. That was 12 years ago, and they are like my own."

—Pat, stepmother of two

"I have a 12-page paper due tomorrow on The Constitutional Convention and I JUST remembered about it! Could you help me? And while you're 'helping' could I play Game Cube?"

They really need you.

"My teenage stepdaughter read a poem at my brother's wedding last year. As I listened to her read, I felt a sense of gratitude toward my family and my friends for embracing her, for finding a role for her not only in the wedding, but in the extended family."

—Meri, stepmother of one

After a while, no one thinks "step" anymore.

154

Your family is *the* family.

155

Chapter Five

Baby Steps

*Stepparenting Infants
and Toddlers*

Little steps may require more of an adult's time and
attention than older children, but the investment is
offset by the benefits of being
involved in someone's life
almost from the start. You will
become part of your stepchild's
earliest memories, watching
him take his first steps and
attending his Joyful Noise
Chorus concerts and
preschool Valentine's Day
parties. Someday you'll
be able to look back and
remember when he said
"wafclosh" instead of
"washcloth" and couldn't

get to sleep without "Bunny Car." Plus, little kids
like to make new friends, especially grown-up ones,
which can mean the transition to fully accepting you
as a stepmom may be short and sweet. One possible
downside: Videotapes of family vacations will include
you, which does mean your clothing and hairstyles
will come under comic scrutiny in future years—
sorry.

156

Little kids don't censor themselves when they speak, so if they don't like the way you make macaroni and cheese, you'll know it. But if they say they love you, they'll mean that too.

157

You didn't have to make any of those agonizing decisions regarding circumcision, vaccinations, or when to cut off the baby curls. You got them as-is.

" As we sat in church recently, my 4-year-old stepson leaned over and put his head on my shoulder. It was so sweet and particularly significant because, of my three stepchildren, he's had the hardest time adjusting to our new family situation. "

—Caroline, mother of two,
stepmother of three

158 **Y**ou can bottle-feed without guilt.

159 **Y**ou will be just detached enough that you won't view every single object in the world in terms of its ability to fit into the baby's mouth.

160 **A**s the backup rocker and soother, you only have to memorize four or five lullabies, not 104.

"Katherine Ellison's *The Mommy Brain* describes numerous scientific studies—some concluded, some still underway—that suggest that when women become mothers, their brains become bigger and actually work better than they did before."

—Susan Konig, writer

161 You have a merely peripheral role in trying to figure out how to dissuade him from dragging around his blankie all the time.

162

You'll discover that there are few things in life more rewarding than making a baby laugh.

163

You learn how to follow orders, as in milk must be in the Snoopy cup, not in the Elmo cup, unless it is chocolate milk, in which case it goes in the cup that has a one-eyed cat on it.

164 You didn't lose a day of your life weeping over the weird first haircut you gave her.

165 You get instructions to follow—"don't feed him strained peas"—without having to go through the projectile vomiting that accompanied the learning process.

"Concerns about children are . . . heavily influenced by nostalgia. Let's not fool ourselves about children's lives in the past. In the 1800s, estimates are that 23 percent of children had lost one or both parents by age 5, 50 percent by age 13, and 70 percent by age 24."

—Susan Gamache, MA, RCC, psychologist and researcher

166 You will be forced to mend the holes in your socks and clean up your language because your little stepperson will undoubtedly share any less-than-flattering informa-tion about you at preschool.

... and sometimes my stepmom puts this bleach stuff on her little moustache so it's kind of invisible and then she puts make-up on her shoulder to cover her snake tattoo...

Online Help!

Here are some Web sites to check out if you need information or support.

www.saafamilies.org
The Stepfamily Association of America is a national, nonprofit organization dedicated to successful stepfamily living.

www.comamas.com
Based on the book *Stepwives: 10 Steps to Help Ex-wives and Stepmothers End the Struggle and Put the Kids First*, this site focuses on teaching "stepwives" how to develop cooperative and respectful relationships.

www.secondwivesclub.com
Women who are in a second marriage or blended family can network with others in similar circumstances on this site.

www.bonusfamilies.com

The Bonus Families® organization is dedicated to the peaceful coexistence between divorced parents and their new families, preferring the word "bonus" to "step," as bonus implies a reward for a job well done.

www.sharekids.com

ShareKids.com is a co-parenting system designed to assist individuals in managing child sharing between homes.

www.yourstepfamily.com

The official online magazine of the Stepfamily Association of America, this e-zine offers stepfamilies solutions, advice, and problem-solving strategies.

"Realize that you won't get recognition for the wonderful things that you do now, but it will pay off much later, when the kids are older and they recognize just how much you've given them."

—John Gray, author

167 Your stepson's insistence on wearing Wonder Woman pajamas is just an interesting little quirk to you, not a reason to make an appointment with a child psychologist.

168 You can take a job as a government code breaker because you were the one who figured out that "roono" was pasta and "kleppo" was kitchen.

" **A**s endless as the days seem now when you're rereading for the millionth time the page where Curious George gets the new bicycle, you'll wake up one morning wishing you could relive them."

— Joyce Maynard, author

" **A** new baby is like the beginning of all things—wonder, hope, a dream of possibilities."

—Eda Le Shan, author

10 Ways Stepparenting Will Change Your Life

1. You'll start spelling words like "nap" and "vegetables."

2. You'll save the empty wrapping paper rolls for "swords."

3. You will have to make sure that the butter is out of reach so that the three-year-old does not use it to make the cat shiny.

4. When you can't find your car keys, you will have to consider the fact that they might have been flushed down the toilet.

5. Your gym bag will have to share trunk space with juice boxes, Goldfish crackers, extra sweatshirts, a box of

Band-Aids, and Colorforms (for unexpected restaurant stops).

6. Before you put in a videotape, you'll need to check to make sure someone hasn't recently tried to "play" a Pop-Tart.

7. You will look in the oven before you turn it on.

8. You will feel compelled to grab the mail as soon as it arrives so that you can take out the Victoria's Secret and Frederick's of Hollywood catalogs.

9. Your first question about a new restaurant will no longer be about the cuisine or the wine selection but about whether it serves chicken nuggets and french fries.

10. You will need to have a ready explanation for certain TV commercials, such as the one about "a wrecked tile this function."

169

You won't obsess over his refusal to eat anything but  pasta shaped like wagon wheels.

170

Your stepdaughter is not expected to learn three new letters on your watch, but if she does, great!

171

Your house will be filled with giggling.

172 Subconsciously, you are collecting stories for the time, years from now, when your stepdaughter says, "Tell me about when I was a baby."

173 You think her attachment to a plastic troll head she found at the park is endearing, not freaky.

Y ou'll never ever be tempted to say, "I suffered through 23 hours of hard labor for *this*?" 174

Y ou can be part of creating a personal family vocabulary that will include your very own made-up names to cover events like passing gas, going to the bathroom, and having something visible in your nose. 175

Y ou're not even mildly tempted to make your own baby food. 176

177

If the clown doesn't show for your stepdaughter's birthday party, you will do your best to make her feel better, but you won't be haunted for decades to come by memories of her sobbing as she tries to blow out the birthday candles.

" **O**ne hundred years from now, it will not matter what my bank account was, how big my house was, or what kind of car I drove. But the world may be a little better because I was important in the life of a child. "

—Forest Witcraft, scholar and teacher

178 You have an excuse to do all sorts of fun things like make Creepy Crawlers, blow bubbles, and make pretend food out of Play-Doh.

179 At Christmastime, you won't be expected to stand in line for seven hours to buy My Little Pony's Wedding Chapel (but if you happen upon one and grab it, you're a hero).

"I had been trying for some time to find a special activity that my young stepdaughter and I could share. She liked the idea of playing Monopoly (she'd watched her older brothers play) but wasn't quite ready for the real thing. So she and I decided to play by special rules she invented. It's really funny—and I like the fact that only the two of us really 'get it.' Everyone else who watches becomes very confused!"

—Meredith, stepmother of four

180 You aren't on the lookout for your family's odd traits— Uncle Doug's Dumbo ears or Cousin Anita's honking laugh, for instance.

Y ou have a legitimate reason to wander around toy stores stroking the stuffed animals and perusing the picture books.

181

A fter she bites a playmate in preschool, you won't be up all night wondering where you went wrong.

182

B ecause you have time to miss them between visits, you can truly appreciate how cute they are.

183

The Best Books to Read with Your Little Steps

Forget about *Cinderella*! More enlightened authors have written stories that show the kinder, gentler side of stepmothers. Here are some books you can proudly read with your little steps:

Sarah, Plain and Tall
by Patricia MacLachlan

When their father invites a mail-order bride to be part of their prairie family, Caleb and Anna are drawn to their new stepmother and hope that she will stay.

No One Is Going to Nashville
by Mavis Jukes

When Sonia finds a stray dog and her father refuses to let her keep him, her stepmother saves the day (and the dog). Funny and upbeat.

My Wicked Stepmother
by Norman Leach

Tom is determined to dislike his new stepmother no matter how well she treats him. But even "wicked" stepmothers can have their feelings hurt. Sweet.

The Memory String
by Eve Bunting

Especially poignant for a child who has lost her mother, this touching story centers around Laura's attachment to a string of buttons, with each button representing an important family memory. When the necklace breaks and buttons are lost, Laura realizes that her new stepmother truly does understand how she is feeling.

Boundless Grace
by Mary Hoffman

Grace travels to Africa to visit her father and his new family, learning that "families are what you make them." Her stepmother plays a peripheral, though positive, role in the story.

184 It's not your job to break the news about Santa.

185 You'll enjoy watching her zip around on her Big Wheel, crashing into trash cans and mowing down the cat, without experiencing her father's haunting visions of the future when she will be driving an actual car.

186 Babies love it when you dance with them, so you can hold the baby close and practice fancy footwork to use with your husband on the dance floor.

187 You didn't earn a reputation in pediatrics for making three middle-of-the-night trips to the emergency room because his bowel movements looked too "lumpy."

188

It won't traumatize you if anyone mistakes your stepson for a girl.

189 You'll realize that finding an inchworm on the ground is much more interesting than finding a dollar bill.

"Outings are so much more fun when we can savor them through the children's eyes."

—Lawana Blackwell, author

190

It won't reflect on you when your 3-year-old stepdaughter announces at a family gathering that she is writing a story and it will be called "My Bagina."

Chapter Six

Next Steps

The Middle Ages

The elementary school years can be the golden years for parents and stepparents—you know their friends, and their friends actually like you; they want you to come to school and help out at the class parties; you can solve nearly all of their problems in five minutes or less. You're beyond teething and tantrums, but haven't hit dreadlocks and dating.

True, they can speak perfectly now, which means they won't hesitate to remind you that you're "not their real mother." And they may have their moments when they wistfully hearken back to when their parents were together—within earshot of you, of course. But they are more likely to accept a new stepparent than a teenager or maybe even an adult stepchild would be.

Despite the challenges, you will feel a tremendous sense of achievement for helping to guide a child into young adulthood. Chances are, someday they will thank you for that.

191 You have little people who want to do fun projects with you, like make clothespin dolls and shoe-box dollhouses.

"This is Isabel, the princess. She is going to have pink hair and a long, fancy dress. She has a stepmother, but a nice one, not a wicked one..."

"Last Mother's Day, I received the most wonderful card from my stepdaughter. She had included a letter that started with 'Reasons I love you,' and she listed everything from making her breakfast and making sure her homework was done to more general things like loving and caring about her. When, a month or so later, my husband got a Father's Day card that just said, 'You're a great dad,' I think he was a bit jealous!"

—Joy, stepmother of two

196 You can replace your gym workout with a vigorous game of capture the flag with the kids (which is more fun anyway).

197 You don't have to be the meanie who says that children shouldn't eat Halloween candy for breakfast.

10 Secrets of Happy Stepmoms

1. Be more like an aunt than a mother. Step back and allow your husband to set and enforce limits (though you do have the right to insist on courtesy and respect).

2. Give yourself permission not to love them right away. And if you never love your stepkids as much as your biological ones, that's okay too.

3. Do what you can to see that the adult relationships stay civil. Refrain from pointing out any similarities between your husband's ex-wife and Cruella De Vil.

4. Make the marriage a priority. Try to see things from your husband's perspective. Back him up in front of the kids. Make time for just the two of you. Remind yourself why you fell in love with him.

5. Don't take things personally. Even if his mom's cookies *are* better than yours, who really cares?

6. Understand the stages of a stepfamily. It won't follow the road map of a biological family. Read up or talk to others who've been there so that your expectations are realistic. Remind yourself often that in second families things get better with time

7. Start special family traditions. Celebrate the winter solstice or Arbor Day with activities that make you feel like a family.

8. Get a life. Garden, kayak, do aerobics, write poetry. Find an activity that will refresh you and give you some perspective on your family life.

9. Laugh together. Your stepson's list of all the gross things he found when he cleaned out your car *is* pretty funny.

rotten tomato that must have rolled out of grocery bag

grubby Goldfish crackers

used Bandaid

1 dirty sock

dog biscuits (even though the dog ran away 2 years ago)

10. Promote and encourage the relationship between your husband and his kids. It's the right thing to do— and all of you will benefit.

198 As the stepmom, you may exempt yourself from discussions about whether last year's lunchbox, backpack, and umbrella are perfectly acceptable or whether your stepdaughter's recent fascination with unicorns is enough to justify replacing said items with their unicorned counterparts.

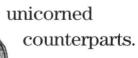

"My stepdaughter, who just started first grade, told me that she wants to take me to school for 'sharing,' the modern-day equivalent of 'show and tell.' I asked her what kinds of things the other kids had brought, and she listed an American Girl doll, a snake skin, a rock collection, and a potato that looked like SpongeBob. I *think* I'm flattered!"

—Shar, mother of two, stepmother of one

Rules for Family Meetings

Family meetings are a great way for stepfamilies to communicate. Creating a forum where family members feel free to discuss concerns and share in decision making makes it less likely that resentments will build. Here are some guidelines for running a successful meeting:

1. Use the family meeting to discuss household rules and chores and to resolve conflicts, as well as to share good news or plan family vacations.

2. Before the meeting, post an agenda and encourage family members to add topics they'd like to discuss.

3. Meet regularly, not just when there's a crisis.

4. Keep meetings short and keep members focused.

5. Make sure everyone has a chance to speak.

6. Encourage courteous listening and respectful speaking.

7. Rotate the role of leader so that everyone has a turn.

8. Try to reach a consensus rather than take a vote, where some members will feel they "lost."

9. Take notes during the meeting and summarize them at meeting's end.

"Although divorce and remarriage may confront families with stresses and adaptive challenges, they also offer opportunities for personal growth and more harmonious, fulfilling family and personal relationships."

— *Journal of Family Psychology* editors
Dr. Mavis Hetherington and
Dr. James H. Bray

You can enjoy these years before the can't-possibly-pay-for-college panic sets in.

199

They are still excited about being in family videos.

200

You know more than they do, something that won't last much longer.

201

202 A home is a friendlier place if there are two Polly Pocket families set up on the coffee table, just waiting for little hands to decide who will visit whom.

203 If you only have the stepkids a few nights a week, you can serve milk shakes after every dinner.

"On those days—and there will be many—when you're trying to remember how you ever thought you loved this guy and his precious little darlings, relax. They all grow up. And when they do, they'll understand and respect you. If you're lucky, they may even love you."

—Kathleen Parker, columnist

204 You may be lucky enough to have wispy hair to braid into pigtails, little fingernails to paint, and dress-up clothes to button and zip.

205 You got to skip baby gymnastics class and rec center toddler play-group. They could already do cartwheels and make friends when you got them.

"**R**ather than enduring the time you spend with his kids, enjoy it. Tell knock-knock jokes, bake cookies, make dioramas—do anything other than withdraw and watch the clock until they leave. . . . Intimacy may be a long time coming, but, like so many other situations in life, you've just got to put in the time."

—**Rosemary Rogers, author**

Ideas for Long-Distance Stepmoms

You can be an involved, available stepparent, even from hundreds of miles away. Here are some ideas:

• E-mail her a brainteaser or riddle one day, then the answer the next.

• Record a book onto a cassette tape, and then send him the tape and the book.

• Have a special day and time set aside when you and your husband will talk to her on the phone (or get an 800 number so that she can call you whenever she'd like).

- Send your stepchild a disposable camera and a large, pre-stamped envelope addressed to you so that as soon as he's used up all the film, he can drop the camera into the envelope and mail it back to you to get the photos developed.

- Write a book together: Take turns writing chapters and mailing or e-mailing them to each other.

- Share experiences by reading the same book, watching the same television series, or going to the same movie and then discussing it afterward by phone or e-mail.

261

"My stepdaughter was trying to teach herself how to write in cursive. She leaned over a paper at the kitchen table writing and writing. When she finally wandered off to watch TV with her brother, I went over to see how she had done. The cursive was pretty crude, but the message she had been trying to write was great: 'I love my new stepmom. I love my new stepmom. I love my new stepmom. . . .'"

—Sally, mother of one,
stepmother of two

Stepfamily Traditions

Family traditions create shared memories and help individuals build a history together. Stepfamilies need to have rituals and traditions that are more flexible to allow for scheduling conflicts. Some step-families get creative and celebrate "new to everyone" occasions like the first day of each season or the last day or week of school. Here are some ideas for traditional holidays, most of which don't require all being together on the actual day.

The New Year: Start a "funniest thing" book. At the start of each new year, have everyone write a short story about the funniest family memory from the past year. Staple them together so that each year you can read the previous year's stories.

Valentine's Day: On construction paper hearts, have everyone write down "The Thing I Love Most About You"—one for each person in the family. The next year, use them to decorate the house for Valentine's Day.

Easter and Passover: Celebrate the coming of spring and new beginnings by planting a tree together in your yard. Every year, take a photo of everyone standing by the same tree.

Thanksgiving: From colored construction paper, cut out one leaf for each person in the family (and anyone who visits over the holiday). Everyone can write down something he or she is

thankful for on a leaf, then sign and date
the back. Afterward, cover each leaf
with clear contact paper and attach
them to a string like a garland. Add to
it (and reread) every year.

Christmas: Make a variety of orna-
ments using photos that represent the
previous year. With each passing year,
your tree will hold more memories for
every member of the family.

"When my husband and I got married, we wanted to start some special holiday traditions, but most of the holidays were already 'taken.' So we decided to do Halloween up really big, starting with selecting pumpkins, then having a carving party at home. We make pumpkin cupcakes, pumpkin soup—any recipe with pumpkins! Now the kids are as excited for our special Halloween as they are for Christmas!"

—Stacie, mother of two, stepmother of one

266

You've moved past the stage where you worry about them drawing all over themselves (or the couch) with permanent marker, swallowing loose change, or dousing the cat with your Chanel N°5.

207 Chances are pretty good that their mother will get stuck with the job of locating two refrigerator boxes and 10 feet of PVC piping for their final project in social studies.

208 Watching your stepdaughter play in her under-12 soccer league, you won't embarrass yourself by making a scene when you realize that

 the goalie for the other team is actually 14.

"I attend every one of my stepson's soccer games without fail. Even though I'd been going for five years, I wasn't sure he was always aware that I was there. One time, though, I had something big come up at work, and I had to stay late. I missed a game. My husband told me that he had come running over to the stands at halftime asking, 'Where's Judy?' So my presence had been noted after all!"

—Judy, mother of one, stepmother of two

Show Your Little Steps the Silver Lining

When one of our flock suffers, we suffer. Much is made of the negative impact of divorce and remarriage on kids, but the benefits are rarely discussed. Remind your kids and stepkids of the blessings that come with being part of a stepfamily:

1. They have a dog at their dad's house and the world's coolest sledding hill at their mom's. Different households offer all sorts of different opportunities.

2. Their parents treasure and appreciate the time they have with them even more now because they are not always together.

3. They learn important coping skills that they will rely on throughout their lives and find inner strength they didn't know they had.

4. They have more people in their world who care about them: not just parent figures, but grandparents, aunts, uncles, and cousins.

5. They develop a true empathy for other people working through personal challenges, making them kinder people and better friends.

Chapter Seven

Big Steps

Life with Tweens and Teens

It can be tough to love your own teenagers, never mind someone else's. When a teenager is slamming doors, grunting rather than speaking, and blasting rap music, most stepmoms can't hearken back to memories of when the same teen was a sweet 6-month-old or a darling toddler. But when kids behave the worst, that's generally when they need caring adults the most. You can play a vital role in the lives of your stepteens by offering guidance and advice (with a little more objectivity than biological parents). By helping your husband parent his tween or teen, you will earn his gratitude—and there'll be a little character building in it for you, too.

If your stepteen is starting to become a real handful, don't hesitate to employ a few stepmom tricks. Watch how fast the kids do your bidding when you threaten to belt out Barry Manilow songs in front of their friends or to wear your T-shirt from 1976 that says, "I'm Kathy. Fly me!"

209 It's easier to be a teenager's friend than a teenager's parent, and stepmothers get to be friends.

210

When you play basketball with your stepson, you don't have to spot him points or play left-handed—he provides some stiff competition!

211

It's likely you'll slide under the radar when it comes to being on the list of parents who are asked to chaperone school dances.

275

212 With teenagers in the house, you never have to worry that a ringing phone will go unanswered.

213 You won't try to keep them little forever, which they'll appreciate.

"I bought my stepson a guitar because I'd heard him talking for months about wanting to teach himself how to play. When I gave it to him, he thanked me, but with a teenager's typical reserve. A few days later, I received the most heartfelt thank-you note from him, ending with 'You make every day brighter for me.' I almost cried."

—Gloria, stepmother of two

"I find that I am a filter between Emma and her dad. She tells me things that her dad should know, aware that I won't overreact and can be a bit more objective. She uses me to test the waters because I'm safer. We decide together how to talk to her dad. I do feel like I fill a void that way."

—Terry, mother of two, stepmother of one

Though you get to sit in the front row and clap when he wins his award at the basketball banquet, you do not need to meet with the principal when he rides around the school parking lot on the hood of his buddy's pickup.

"I didn't really expect my new stepchildren to give me Mother's Day gifts, but the two boys bought me flowers and took me to breakfast. My younger stepdaughter made me a beautiful card, and the older one gave me the best gift of all—a hug and a very genuine 'thank you.'"

—Denise, stepmother of four

215

You are free to watch *CSI* while your husband is forced to continue the conversation with his son about why he will not buy him a BB gun or an ATV for his birthday.

216

You can enjoy a high school lacrosse game without suffering the misery of a biological parent: agony when she's on the bench and fear of fatal injury when she's on the field.

217 You only have to live through an occasional morning of your stepdaughter freaking out while trying to put in her contact lenses or cover a pimple.

218 When your stepson remembers (at 10:20 p.m.) that he needs to print out a 10-page research paper and then discovers that the printer is out of ink, you can roll over in bed guilt-free while your husband puts on his clothes and heads to Staples.

"Being in a stepfamily is like being part of an extended family. When it works well, it gives the child more people to draw from for support and life experience. The stepfamily is the fastest-growing family type in America today, and it's vital to the future of this country that these new families are successful."

—Patricia L. Fry and Judith Mize, authors

" Children need love,
especially when they do
not deserve it. "

—Harold Hulbert , author

" Character cannot be
developed in ease and
quiet. "

—Helen Keller

Teens in a Nutshell

I n case you're new to teens (and your own teen years are long gone), here's an overview of your stepteen's life:

Where he goes: out.

What he does: nothing.

What he is: bored.

What he wants: the car keys.

Why he comes home: to shower and change.

219 Without that genetic link, the kids tend not to embarrass you as much as they embarrass their biological parents. You, in turn, probably don't embarrass them as much as their biological parents do.

"On a recent shopping trip, my teenage stepdaughter and I decided to buy matching sneakers—and neither one of us is embarrassed to wear them!"

—Beth, mother of three, stepmother of two

"Give your teen some space to develop a relationship at his or her own pace. The end result will be greater acceptance, less fighting and ultimately a much better chance at a tranquil step-family life."

—Dr. Susan Bartell, psychologist

10 Little Things That Will Make a Big Difference

It's easy to take positive steps toward bonding with your stepteens. The key is to make them slow and steady steps. Here are some simple ideas to improve relations:

1. Invite their friends to dinner.

2. Ask for their opinions on big things like global warming and little things like the new kitchen curtains.

3. E-mail them a compliment now and then.

4. If you need to correct them, do it with humor and affection.

5. Buy tickets to a special event for the kids and their dad.

6. Make their favorite cookies.

7. Celebrate small triumphs: soccer goals, debate team victories, an "A" on a research paper.

8. Display their photos prominently. Ditto artwork and report cards.

9. Respect their privacy.

10. Say "yes" whenever you can. Save "no" for health and safety issues.

Your stepteens will see to it that your younger kids are up on the latest cool music, cool video games, and cool cargo pants.

You're not responsible for having the "it's time to start using a razor/deodorant/acne cream" conversation.

220

221

222

A s the stepmom, you just see a kid trudging to school. Your husband, however, sees a kid who didn't study for his biology test, splashing through puddles in his brand new $95

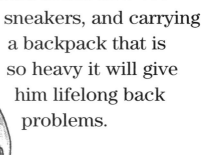

sneakers, and carrying a backpack that is so heavy it will give him lifelong back problems.

"When my teenage stepson went on a weeklong school trip, we gave him spending money so he could buy himself a little something. When he got back from the trip, he proudly showed us what he'd spent the money on: two souvenir spoons for my collection. I was really touched."

—Trinese, mother of four, stepmother of three

"I care very much about my teenage stepchildren and what happens in their lives, but because I didn't create them, I don't feel personally wounded if they make poor or odd choices now and again. I think I have a healthy degree of objectivity and am able to helpfully guide my husband when he struggles with them."

—Leigh, mother of two, stepmother of two

Y ou can return him to his
mom on Sunday evening,
just before the term-paper-
due-Monday panic sets in.

223

Y ou don't have to decide
what orthodontics plan
is best.

224

T he telemarketers may
actually give up on you
because your phone
line will always
be busy.

225

295

How Did *You* Bond with *Your* Teen Step?

- "I took my stepchildren to an American Idols concert. It was their first 'real' concert, and they couldn't stop talking about it."

- "I let my stepdaughter drive my car as soon as she got her learner's permit. I have a bit more patience than her dad, so she liked driving with me."

- "As a science teacher, I was able to give my stepchildren help with their science homework. We always ended up talking about a lot more than just science."

- "When my stepdaughter started considering colleges, I took her to visit my alma mater. We toured the campus together and stopped by my old dorm. It was a nice experience to share."

- "As he approached 16, my stepson was very interested in looking at used cars. On 'our' weekends, I'd let him make appointments with people selling cars, and then I'd drive him around to check them out. We had lots of time to talk together as we drove."

- "My stepson and I went to garage sales together. He loved them more than I did!"

• "I asked my stepdaughter if she would teach me how to play racquetball. Now we play together about once a month."

• "I taught my stepson to cook!"

• "My stepson does quite a bit of volunteer work through our church. I try to arrange my schedule so that I can go with him. I feel good about what we're doing, not just the fact that we're doing it together."

"But a trip to the tanning salon is a NECESSITY! I need a tan like I need HAIR EXTENSIONS and TEETH BLEACHING! How can you say it's a LUXURY item? Do you understand 16-year-old girls at ALL?"

Whether a trip to the tanning salon should be covered by a weekly allowance is not yours to determine.

226

299

227 Mothers have to pretend that *The Scarlet Letter* is a great read; stepmoms can say that it was a snoozer.

228 You don't have to take away her false eyelashes, stiletto heels, or fake nails. Her mom gets to do that.

When your husband flips out because his "baby" was spotted making out at a school dance with a "hottie" (as reported by her older brother), you won't feel like gagging, just giggling.

"Humor is the great thing, the saving thing. The minute it crops up, all our irritations and resentments slip away and a sunny spirit takes their place."

—Mark Twain

Teen *Jeopardy!*

A re you ready to parent teenagers? Take this *Jeopardy!* challenge and find out!

- Reason to stay home from school for two days.

    What is a pimple?

- Reason to stay home from school for two years.

    What are braces?

- Cell phones, 2:00 a.m. curfews, tattoos, and credit cards.

    What do all the other kids have?

- A driver's test.

    What is the only test he'll study for this year?

- The teacher had a weird lisp; the kid who sat next to him hummed to himself and made it hard to concentrate; and he lent his calculator to this really cute girl who never gave it back.

  What are the reasons he got a "D" in algebra?

- Twizzlers, Cheez-Its, and Diet Coke.

  What does your "vegetarian" stepdaughter's diet consist of?

- Four hours of squealing, five towels stained with red hair dye, and no access to the telephone.

  What do you get when Meagan comes over?

- Sleep.

  What do they like to do at 1:00 p.m. that they don't like to do at 1:00 a.m.?

"OK, people, listen up...
Dad, lose the comb-over. And
take off that green jacket.
You look like a bush.
Once you get to school,
no boring everybody
with the story about
seeing Billy Joel in the
airport or your
almost-hole-in-one.
Nancy, your dress
is OK, but those
are granny shoes. Go
for the sandals.
Oh, and don't
laugh. You sound
like a chicken
when you laugh.
OK! Let's head
out!"

230 You won't have to worry about what to wear in public. Your teen will give you detailed instructions on acceptable clothing options as well as specific rules on how to behave.

231

If you have teenage stepsons, you can experiment in the kitchen because they will eat just about anything.

232

You get to accompany them down the black diamond ski runs without having had to endure all those years on the bunny slope.

"Whenever I make Chicken Parmesan, my 17-year-old stepson puts his arms around me and tells me he loves me. I think he means he loves the chicken, but that's great too!"

—Sandy, mother of four, stepmother of two

Making conversation isn't really an issue because teenagers have headphones welded to their ears about 80 percent of the time. (The other 20 percent is spent in the bathroom.)

234 You'll get to use that college essay writing expertise a few more times.

"Rule Number 1 is, don't sweat the small stuff. Rule Number 2 is, it's all small stuff. And if you can't fight and you can't flee, flow."

—Robert S. Eliot, MD

Celebrity Stepchild *When Abraham Lincoln was young, his stepmother, Sarah, encouraged his reading and his studious habits, and prodded his father to do the same. Lincoln described Sarah as "good and kind" and said, "All that I am or hope to be I owe to my angel mother."*

"Sometimes the greatest asset of a step relationship is its distance from the biological relationship. A step relationship can offer a more neutral perspective during highly emotional times. For example, this distance can sometimes allow teens to talk about things they are not quite ready to address with their biological parent."

—Susan Gamache, MA, RCC, psychologist and researcher

235

Teenagers aren't crazy about adults in general, including their biological parents, so you're not at that much of a disadvantage.

236

You can buy him the CD he wants for his birthday knowing that his stereo system with the really big speakers is at his mom's house.

311

"The best thing I did was to read a few books on teen development. Knowing what is 'normal' behavior for the teen years helped me to understand that I shouldn't take a sullen or moody attitude personally."

—Karen, stepmother of two

"Without a doubt, the adolescent years are the hardest time to form a stepfamily."

—Susan Wisdom, author and counselor

You do not have to make those pesky decisions for your stepteen, like whether he should buy back-to-school supplies in August when everyone else seems to, or wait until the second day of school when the teachers actually say what the kids need but the stores are already out of everything.

How to Interpret a Teenager's Facial Expressions

surprised

bored

delighted

worried

angry

horrified

"**M**y 13-year-old stepson went looking for video games at a tag sale in the neighborhood, but he came home with something for me—a mirrored shelf ornament! It's nothing I would have bought for myself, but because it came from him, I absolutely love it!"

—Darlene, mother of three, stepmother of three

238 You're not responsible for coming up with compelling reasons to make your stepson pull up his enormous pants so that the waistband is in the vicinity of his actual waist. (And if you want to buy him pants for his birthday, you don't need to get the size exactly right.)

SIZE LARGE-ISH

"Sometimes . . . new step-parents are able to play peacemaker. . . . As a new adult [who] can approach the situation as a friend and confidant, you may be able to reach a child who is looking to overcome the past. You may be able to intervene and calm the troubled waters. . . ."

—Karon Goodman, author

239 Rather than joining your husband in a meltdown when your stepson shows up with a pierced ear, you see it as an opportunity to pass along all of those earrings-without-mates that you've saved in your jewelry box.

3 Things Cool Stepmoms Don't Do

1. Don't bring veggies and dip or fruit kabobs to a school event. Go for gooey brownies or chocolate chip cookies instead. Let a "real" mother be the sacrificial healthy snack person.

2. Don't try to play hacky sack, learn how to use video-game controls, or put on in-line skates for the first time in front of anyone your stepteen knows or might ever come in contact with.

3. Don't get all Martha Stewart if your stepteens ask for help covering their textbooks. They just want brown paper bag covers that will look like every other kid's books, not something that screams, "My stepmother is crafty!"

240 You won't get freaked out when your stepson gets a man voice and starts shaving.

241 You'll end up with only half of her stuff when she needs a place to store her college things for the summer.

242 If your 16-year-old stepson starts dating an 18-year-old girl, you might raise an eyebrow, but you won't call the police.

"My stepson and I have had the same exchange for the past few years: I will tell him that I love him, and he will say, 'Yeah, I know.' The other day I was dropping him off at school, and he said, 'Thanks Colleen,' and then he added: 'I love you, ya know.' And I said, 'Yeah, I know.'"

—Colleen, stepmother of two

243 In a pinch, you can borrow your teenage stepdaughter's perfume. Ditto her turquoise choker and cute black sandals.

244 You are spared the trauma of signing the waiver when he wants to take hang-gliding lessons or go bungee jumping.

"My two stepdaughters and I started a tradition we call 'Girls' Night In.' We paint each other's finger- and toe-nails, experiment with weird hairdos, order Chinese takeout, and watch a silly TV show or a movie they have chosen. Having our own special tradition—just us girls—has been wonderful."

—Maryanne, mother of one, stepmother of two

"My husband and I coach my stepdaughter's travel soccer team. As we were getting ready for practice one day, I wove my hair into a French braid. My stepdaughter watched me, then asked if I would do that to her hair. Afterward, when we were examining our matching braids, she said, 'I'm lucky that you are my stepmom.'"

—Trina, stepmother of two

W hen they hug you, it's
genuine, not out of habit.

245

. . . .

T he things you most love
in your husband begin
showing up in his kids as they
get older.

246

Chapter Eight

Giant Steps

*When Your Little Steps Are
Finally Grown*

Bigger is often better. Not only have your stepkids
passed the stage where they bring free kittens home
from the county fair and give only three seconds'
notice when they *have* to use the bathroom, they've
also gone through the rebellious stage and settled
nicely into adulthood.

Parenting doesn't stop when children grow
older, but it does change. And it's a lot easier for a
stepparent to accept the change than it is for the
biological parent, who often sees the 5-year-old
rather than the 25-year-old.

You may even be blessed with more grandchildren, courtesy of your stepkids. The older you
get, the more you will appreciate a larger circle of
affection.

247 You do not have to go through your husband's ex-wife to "arrange" a visit with your grown-up steps.

248 When it comes to grandkids, you're not the backup grandma, you're just the grandma.

249 You're no longer mortified by the way they dress . . . and vice versa.

"You can grandparent other people's grandchildren. It's not only biological. . . . To me, . . . it's the roles grandparents play . . . the nurturing teacher, role model, hero, spiritual guide."

—Dr. Arthur Kornhaber,
psychiatrist and author

250 No more piano recitals!

251 You can relax a bit more in front of your adult stepchildren—if you slip in a "damn" or if they see you a bit tipsy, you won't worry that you have caused irreparable harm.

"I married my husband when his sons were teenagers. They really gave us a run for our money, especially the younger one. But now that he's married himself, we can laugh about the chaos of those years. And I know he is sorry for what he put us through."

—Martha, stepmother of two

"It is not necessary for the elderly parent to be biologically related to the 'child' to experience a sense of kinship and intimacy. A stepchild whose parent remarried in early life may view the stepparent as mother or father by the time that person has reached old age; the 'step' aspect to the relationship is less meaningful after forty years than it was after four months."

—Karen L. Fingerman, author

Celebrity Stepchild *"From time to time, Mom 2 . . . still acts like my mother, treating me as if I were her 12-year-old son,"* said Peter Fonda of his stepmother, Susan Blanchard. *"I think it's a riot, and I love her for it; after all, she has been my mother for more than 40 years."*

252 Eating out with adult stepchildren is a lot more fun than it was with little ones. And they might even pick up the bill.

253 They aren't embarrassed to be seen at the movies with you.

254 You won't be up until 3:15 a.m. on Christmas Eve assembling a bicycle, train set, or puppet theater.

"Recently, I bumped into my ex-husband in town, and he shared some sad news about his father. I was standing next to him, wiping away tears, when my 20-year-old stepson happened to walk by with a group of friends. He excused himself and immediately came over to see if I was all right. I could tell he was prepared to defend me if my ex-husband was giving me a hard time!"

—Sharon, mother of one,
stepmother of two

255 Your grown-up steps appreciate the fact that if they aren't able to see their dad on his birthday, you will make sure he has a great day.

256 Now you can keep a dish of candy in the living room (and bottles of beer and wine in the fridge).

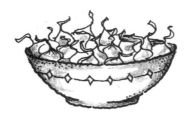

"It took me years to trust my stepmother, Jill—to understand that my dad could love us both, and to lose the chip on my shoulder. Now that I am a stepmother myself, Jill has helped me through some rough times, reminding me that someday my stepson will feel the same about me that I feel about Jill."

—Gabriella, stepmother of one

Celebrity Stepchild *When race car driver Dale Earnhardt Jr. won the Winston Cup in July of 2001, he dedicated it to his stepmother, Teresa, and to his father, who had died in an earlier race. Years before, the elder Earnhardt had acknowledged that while he pursued his career "Teresa raised [the children]."*

"My oldest stepdaughter wouldn't speak to me right after her dad and I eloped. So it meant a lot to me when, some months later, she came to me and said, 'I want to thank you for making my father so happy.'"

—Tessa, mother of three, stepmother of three

What Adult Stepkids Know That Little Steps Don't

- Relationships are complicated; no one is the hero and no one is the villain.

- The negative things their mom told them about you or about their dad are not true.

- Being a stepparent is often a difficult job, and they didn't appreciate you enough when they were younger.

- After getting to know them, you consciously chose to take them into your intimate circle and become their stepmom.

- You gave their father a second chance at a happy, loving marriage.

Celebrity Stepchild *"I think he blamed me in the early years. I was like the evil step-mother. . . . Actually, we really grew to like each other a lot, but we grew to love each other as adults."*

—Shirley Jones, on her stepson, David Cassidy

"Every summer, my husband and I organize a Cousins Camp where my children and stepchildren are invited to drop off their children with us for a week of fun and games. It's crazy, but we enjoy it, and it has cemented the bonds among our children's children."

—Sylvia, mother of three, stepmother of two

257

When the phone rings, you no longer have to worry that it's someone asking you to coach a soccer team, chaperone a field trip to the fire station, or bake four dozen cookies for a student council bake sale.

258

You rediscover your marriage after the kids grow up and move on.

343

259 Now that the kids visit you one at a time instead of in a group, you'll get to know each one better.

...So you ALWAYS wanted to be an OPERA SINGER? I didn't know that!

260 All the child support has been paid, and the custody battles are really over. Whew.

344

"When the youngest of our six combined kids turned 18 last year, my husband and I congratulated ourselves! We felt a real sense of accomplishment."

—Cheryl, mother of three, stepmother of three

261 Instead of helping your stepkids with homework, now you can ask your adult steps for help setting up your DVD player or figuring out your digital camera.

"Open the lid of top and smoothen two number five cells. Invert and poke as you please. Because the screws."

I'm so glad you're helping! I don't even understand the directions!

"It wasn't until my stepdaughter had a baby of her own that she told me how much she appreciated the time and energy that I put into raising her. She also said that the relationship between her dad and me was her ideal, what she hoped she and her husband could achieve. That made me feel wonderful."

—Jackie, mother of two, stepmother of two

"When we were a newer family, I used to feel a bit uncomfortable telling people that we were a stepfamily. But many years later, I feel a sense of accomplishment at being part of a large, diverse family."

—Grace, mother of three, stepmother of four

Older and Wiser Stepmom Wishes

- "I wish I'd had more realistic expectations. I wish I'd read books about stepfamilies and talked with other stepmoms before I got married."

- "I wish my husband and I had spoken to a family therapist as we struggled through the first few years."

- "I wish I'd tried to see life through the eyes of my husband and my stepchildren more often."

- "I wish I'd forgiven the little things more easily."

- "I wish I hadn't started off treating my stepchildren as guests, but as members of the family."

- "I wish we'd had more family meetings so that lingering issues would have been resolved more quickly."

- "I wish I had taken more of a supporting role from the start so that my husband would have been a more hands-on parent."

- "I wish we'd moved into a new home together after we got married so no one felt like an 'intruder.'"

- "I wish I'd tried harder to get along with my husband's ex-wife—or at least refused to let her get under my skin."

- "I wish I had focused more on what I had, rather than what I didn't have."

- "I wish I'd had a more positive image of stepfamilies and stepmothers so that I could have envisioned myself as courageous—a pioneer."

" A friend of mine whose stepkids are now grown gave me great advice. She told me to accept the relationships with my stepchildren for what they are, not continually focus on what I'd like the relationships to be. "

—Debbie, stepmother of two

"We did it. We survived—but more than that—our lives have been given a depth and texture that would not have been possible without our mixed family."

—Karen Savage, author

Now that they're grown, it's a lot more likely that you and your step-children will agree as to what constitutes music.

262

When your stepchild turns out to be a happy, productive adult, a loving spouse, and a responsible parent, you can feel a bit of pride at being part of that.

263

Chapter Nine

Grown and Gone

Becoming a Stepmom When His Kids Are Adults

When you marry a man whose children are grown, you have the luxury of establishing unique adult relationships with your stepkids. As an "intimate outsider," you offer a special kind of parenting— less judgmental and more objective. You are likely to view them as peers, to treat them as the adults they are rather than the children their birth parents remember so well.

Your stepchildren, who may be engaged with their own young families, are more likely to view you with appreciation and kindness, as someone who will love and care for their father as he grows older, rather than as an intruder. And if they are unkind, you'll find it much easier to ignore bad behavior than a younger stepmom who doesn't have the life experience and wisdom to put it all in perspective (and you won't have to see them every other weekend if you don't want to).

With the major parental obligations behind you and no ex-spouses calling regularly, your marriage can develop much more like a young, first marriage does. You will have lots of time for each other. Enjoy.

264 Y ou can watch old family videos without worrying that you'll suddenly appear on-screen with flabby thighs or a hairdo that will send everyone into hysterics.

265 W hen your stepson decides to take piano lessons at age 30, you won't be tempted to remind him that he refused to practice when he was 8.

In their research, Susan Lanspery and Barbara Vinick found that "when husbands' biological children were hostile or unaccepting of them, stepmothers made efforts to reach out, to dissipate hostility, and to establish friendly contact. As time went by, they urged husbands to keep in contact with their children, reminded them to call, issued invitations, or took the lead in communicating with stepchildren themselves."

266 You won't lose sleep when your stepchildren decide to homeschool their children and raise them as Wiccans.

267 If your stepson chooses a career path your husband finds unacceptable, you can be the wise one to say, "A happy carpenter is preferable to an unhappy stockbroker."

"When my stepdaughter got into the law school that was at the top of her list, I was the first one she called. She'll never know what that meant to me."

—Cara, stepmother of two

When your stepchildren decide to get married, being "dad's wife" suddenly sounds better than being the "mother-in-law."

8 Promises to Make to Your Adult Stepchildren

1. I will honor and respect the relationships that came before my entrance into the family.

2. I won't make significant changes to your childhood home right away.

3. I will be understanding if you miss a holiday or special occasion because of other family commitments.

4. I will call before I visit you, or wait to be invited.

5. Rather than offer advice, I'll offer practical help, like running errands or babysitting for your children.

6. I'll accept the rules of your household.

7. I'll do what I can to foster your relationship with your dad.

8. I'll always be there for you.

"I have your groceries and the diapers... Would you like me to hold the baby so you can rest?"

269 Your stepdaughter appreciates that you see her as an accomplished advertising executive, not the bratty baby of the family.

270 When the kids call in the middle of *Desperate Housewives*, you can graciously and quickly pass the phone to their dad so you don't miss a single, delicious moment.

"An estimated 500,000 people older than 65 remarry each year in the United States and since most of them have an average of two children, their unions create 2 million adult stepchildren."

—Jane Glenn Haas, author

271 When your stepson brings his fiancée over to meet you, he will appreciate the fact that you don't have any embarrassing "when he was a little boy" stories to share.

As a stepmom, it's easier to let them make the mistakes they need to in order to learn those all-important life lessons.

272

Your stepdaughter's prospective husbands won't be sizing you up as an indication of what's in store for them 20 years down the road.

273

As newer members of the family, you and your stepdaughters-in-law will feel a special kinship.

274

"I made a real effort to connect with the family of my stepdaughter's fiancé. We have invited them to various holiday parties and family gatherings. I know my stepdaughter appreciates it. Once you have pulled a stepfamily together, it's easy to widen the circle."

—Allison, mother of four, stepmother of two

275

If your stepdaughter can't locate the still life that she painted in third grade and that won a blue ribbon, you can't be blamed for tossing it.

276

You may tear up at graduations, but you won't embarrass yourself by sobbing so hard you have to go to the ladies' room.

Adult-Proofing Your Home

Just about every new mom knows that she must baby-proof her house with locks on kitchen cabinets and plugs in the outlets. The same concept holds true for setting boundaries for visiting adult stepkids. The goal is to protect your personal belongings and your privacy while still making everyone feel welcome.

- Place cute "*Do Not Disturb*" signs on private rooms like your office so that personal papers or bills aren't moved or perused.

- Provide a drawer for each grandchild so that, instead of taking home their favorite toys (and depleting your supply), you can suggest they "hide" special things in their drawers.

- Once you've read a magazine or book, add it to a reading basket for adult family members who can select anything of interest to read at your house or to take home with them.

- Establish an "ask first" rule for the garage so that you don't discover one winter morning that your extra bottles of windshield washer fluid have disappeared.

- A basket of extra mittens, hats, flip-flops, T-shirts, and sweatshirts will keep people from poking through your closet to find what they need.

277 You probably won't get any weepy, middle-of-the-night calls from your postpartum stepdaughter, but you *will* get to bounce the new baby on your knee.

278 Your family tree won't be permanently mangled if your newly married stepson trades the family name for a hyphenated last name invented by his bride.

The kids won't tease you about your past phases: the belly-dancing phase, the guitar-lessons phase, or the learning-to-speak-German phase.

"Ich würde bitte einen einzigartigen und anderen Hotelraum weil Zimmer von mir scheußlich Schlecht fordern."

Translation:
"I would please demand a unique and other hotel space because room of mine is nasty bad."

280 If your step-daughter drops out of medical school to join PETA, you'll find it inter-esting and inspiring rather than misguided or tragic.

281 Because you weren't there for the sibling rivalry stuff, you're not waiting for them to relapse when they visit.

"The high success rate of the fifty-something [stepmother] seemed commensurate with her increased self-confidence and her accumulation of life experience. Nothing really surprises women in their fifties. . . ."

—Perdita Kirkness Norwood, author

"Adult children can play a very positive role in the stepfamily. They can make younger children feel more secure and add continuity to a stepfamily."

—Barbara Mullen Keenan, author

"It's freeing when your stepchildren are adults. You no longer have to let unacceptable behavior go because you are afraid that if you discipline them, they will be traumatized."

—Suzanne, mother of one, stepmother of two

You won't be tempted to create a shrine to a child who has moved away.

282

375

283 While their biological parents have to make the shift from managing their kids' lives to just offering the occasional bit of advice, you're already there.

"I made an effort to find an activity to share with each of my adult stepkids. My older stepdaughter and I are decorating a dollhouse together, and my younger stepdaughter and I are taking classes to learn how to bake bread."

—Barb, stepmother of two

284 Most adults bond with just about anyone who shows their children affection and attention, so the three hours you spend making Play-Doh food with the grandkids will really pay off.

When everyone gets together, there's no lapsing into old family roles, because you are a new family.

285

"My stepdaughter asked me to babysit for her toddler when she was in her friend's wedding—and I was her first choice!"

—Sandy, mother of two, stepmother of one

"**B**ecause I am considerably younger than my husband, I have children who are about the same age as the children of my oldest stepchild, Tara. We have a great relationship and are very supportive of one another. I don't know what I'd do without her."

—Amanda, mother of two, stepmother of three

Your stepchildren don't subconsciously expect you to fulfill every need they have (the way they expect their biological parents to).

286

When the going gets tough, the tendency will be for them to move back into their mother's basement rather than yours.

287

A grown-up stepchild knows what it's like to want the family to bless a new relationship.

288

Chapter Ten

In Step with Your Husband

*Making Your Marriage
the Priority*

Remarriage has been called the triumph of hope
over experience. Having lived through the trauma
of a failed first marriage, you choose to enter into
a second marriage determined to avoid repeating
past mistakes—to do it right this time.

Many women are surprised to find that
second marriages that include children from prior
relationships follow a completely different road
map than first marriages do. A second marriage
that involves children does not necessarily have a
honeymoon period—right from the start, you may
be coping with a resentful ex-wife, children who
refuse to accept you, and a husband whose loyalties
are divided. Initially, his bond with his children may

be stronger than his bond with you, creating conflict and jealousy. Unlike first marriages, in which marital satisfaction tends to decline over time, in second marriages, the greatest discontent often comes early on.

The good news: studies show that in second marriages, relationships steadily improve. So if you can manage today, you'll be in great shape a year from today. And a good marriage provides your kids and his with a model of what marriage should be, making it more likely that they will have the tools to create successful relationships of their own.

289 Stepparenting forces you and your husband to work closely as a team, the way Tonto and the Lone Ranger have to stick together when they're surrounded by outlaws.

Doing things for each other's children is the ultimate loving gesture and never goes unnoticed and unappreciated.

Thanks for taking Joey to karate! ♡

290

The more kids you leave behind, the more fun you'll have at a couples-only resort. It's a proven scientific theorem.

291

292 Because of the chaos of your lives, you are forced to consciously create "honeymoon moments."

"It is hard to find couple time when you are stepparents because you both tend to hyperparent out of guilt. My husband and I try to repackage daily events and errands into 'dates.' We'll get groceries and then stop for lunch, or run to Home Depot and then follow it with a trip to the gym together. We take advantage of every minute we can be doing something together."

—Kate, mother of two, stepmother of four

293 You have to start from scratch and scrutinize everything, from the way you handle school functions to your holiday traditions. But reevaluating the patterns and habits you've fallen into can be very worthwhile—you may find that there are a number of ways you can do things differently to make your life easier and better.

Celebrity Stepmom *According to Joanne Woodward, "sexiness wears thin after a while and beauty fades, but to be married to a man who makes you laugh every day, ah, now that's a real treat!" She has been married to Paul Newman for 45 years. Together they have six children. But did you know that three of those six children were from Paul's first marriage to Jacqueline Witte?*

"Once you realize that sustained happiness is not something you should expect from marriage, you can be very happy. Most people . . . have imperfect marriages. . . . If you have friendship, respect, commitment, emotional intimacy, and sexual crackle, you've got 99 percent of what you need to go the distance. You never get all you need from a marriage. . . . Connect with what you love to do and plug into your personal passions."

—Iris Krasnow, author

294

Good marriages are strengthened as each spouse makes small sacrifices to accommodate the other; in a stepfamily, there are limitless opportunities for the husband and wife to help one another and to become closer.

"The more you invest in a marriage, the more valuable it becomes."

—Amy Grant, singer

295 In a second marriage, both spouses are forced early on to see the world through the other's eyes.

296 You get to know each other quickly and deeply when children are part of the package.

Hey Dad, would you burp the alphabet for me like you used to? And then would you make that funny noise with your nose and your comb?

The World According to Your Husband

As challenging as your stepmom role is, being a stepdad isn't without its difficulties. If you are able to understand some of your husband's fears and concerns (and make yours known to him), you will be able to empathize with each other and feel more connected. Here's what he may be thinking:

- Not only does he miss seeing his kids every day, he feels guilty that he moved out.

- He worries about the influence his ex-wife has over his kids. Even though he knows it upsets you, he sometimes needs to placate her to alleviate a little of his anxiety.

- He feels the financial pressure of helping to support two families.

- He is jealous of the bond that you have with your kids.

- He often feels torn between your needs and wishes and those of his kids.

- He is aware of the irony that he lives with your children (who may resent his presence) and doesn't live with his own (who wish they could see him more often).

- He's not sure how to be a stepfather. Is he supposed to teach his stepson to play catch, or is that stepping on the "real" dad's toes?

- He feels helpless when your ex-husband gives you a hard time because he knows that if he interferes it's likely to make matters worse.

- He feels frustrated that he can't discipline your children; it makes him feel powerless.

- If his ex-wife remarried, he is sad that his kids are connecting every day with another "dad" (while he is paying the bills through child support).

297 You appreciate the appealing parenting traits in your spouse that you didn't find in your first husband.

298 In the case of stepfamilies, familiarity breeds content.

299 With lots of kids' schedules to accommodate, you have to work together right from the start. There's no you-go-your-way-and-I'll-go-mine.

"I think my husband and I love each other more deeply because we know how hard the other has worked to bond with the stepchildren."

—Suzanne, mother of four, stepmother of three

"The key to success is . . . remembering that the more you give away, the more you have."

—Christopher Reeve

"**I** am in awe of my husband's patience with all of the kids. I know that his job demands patience, but I don't see him in that setting. I fall in love with him all over again when he is able to quietly diffuse a situation that is starting to make me crazy."

—Stephanie, mother of one,
stepmother of two

300

Even though at times you may feel that your children are pulling you in opposite directions, focusing on the experiences and emotions that you have in common quickly draws you back together as a couple.

301 Seeing how quickly and easily your kids make up after a spat may show you and your husband a thing or two about forgiving and forgetting.

"The emotional well-being of . . . a family is directly tied to the quality of the parents' relationship. Make a happy marriage a priority, and the pay-off for your children is huge."

—Margaret Renkl, writer

400

When you finally, finally have an evening without the kids, you're as giddy and excited as teenagers whose parents are out for the evening.

302

You start off a bit wiser, having learned lessons from the first time around.

303

You are offering your children and stepchildren the opportunity to have a close-up look at a solid, successful marriage.

304

305 Because you have to be somewhat secretive with your affection, making out has the thrill it did when you were in high school.

"**S**econd marriages that involve kids are tough. I think both people spend a lot more time assessing the overall situation than in first marriages. You constantly ask yourself the question, 'Is this worth it?' And every time you answer, 'Yes it is,' you solidify the relationship."

—Liz, mother of one, stepmother of three

"The happiest couples have found a way to fit rituals into their lives—even if they have children. And research shows that happily married people are healthier, happier, richer, and live longer."

—William J. Doherty, PhD,
author and psychologist

How We Stay Connected

Making couple time a priority is critical because the success of the stepfamily hinges on the strength of the marriage. If you find the time to argue, you can find the time to connect.

- "Unless it's pouring rain, we take a walk during our lunch hour every day. Some days, it's the only uninterrupted hour we have together. It's good for us physically as well as emotionally."

- "We clear our calendars on Monday nights and drive to a nearby theater where we can see a movie for two dollars each. Even though the movies are not always ones we would have

chosen, we've been pleasantly
surprised on a couple of occasions,
and at the very least, there's lots to
talk about on the ride home."

• "We take dancing lessons on Sunday
nights. It's an easy night for us both
to take a couple of hours away from
home, and we usually end up in
hysterics as neither of us seems to
be much of a dancer."

• "Even though I'm new to golf, my
husband and I signed up for a couples
golf league that plays every Tuesday
night. I'm flattered that my husband
is eager to play with me when a lot
of guys would rather play with their
buddies."

• "We bought a tandem bicycle, and we
committed to riding it three times a
week. It's great because even if we

are miffed at each other, we're stuck working together on the bicycle so it helps us get back in sync."

• "We leave lovey-dovey Post-It notes for each other everywhere. We have such busy schedules that there are days when that is our primary form of communication."

• "After dinner is coffee-without-kids time. The kids head upstairs to do homework or play, and my husband and I linger over coffee and dessert and share the day's news."

"**O**ur lives are made up of thousands of small, insignificant moments. When we put all the moments together, they create our relationships."

—Anne O'Connor, psychologist

In their landmark NIH study, Dr. James H. Bray and John Kelly found that "when a marriage works in a stepfamily, it often works especially well."

A relationship that is cemented not only by shared joy but also by shared challenges and sorrows is a stronger one with deeper roots.

It's never been truer that what doesn't break you as a couple will make you stronger.

308 Marrying a man when either of you has children means that you've made a deeper commitment to him than if you had no kids. Children sometimes provide the motivation you need to make the marriage work.

309 If you plan your "dates" for the right weekends, you have free babysitters—the exes!

"My husband and I have a 'Brady Bunch' family. We had found a few minutes of peace and quiet one summer day in our hammock. We were talking quietly when some of the younger kids began to approach us. His oldest son and my oldest daughter stopped them and in hushed tones told them to let us have some time alone together. We were very impressed with their thoughtfulness."

—Patty, mother of three,
stepmother of three

310 Being a successful stepparent means developing traits that will make you a better spouse: tolerance, compassion, patience, and the ability to provide unconditional love.

"If there is one primary source of strength for a stepmother, it is a good marriage."

—Karen Savage and Patricia Adams, authors

Marriage Armor

It is often the marriage that takes the hardest hit during visits by the stepkids. You silently resent the intrusion and inevitable turmoil that come with the visits, and your husband is anxious to reconnect with his kids without upsetting you. Here are some tips to protect your marriage:

• Rather than ignoring problems, develop strategies together ahead of time to cope with recurring issues.

• Encourage your husband to take extra time to connect with his kids when they first arrive and as they are about to leave. If this means that you take his turn doing the dinner dishes, that's okay.

- Plan a few flexible family activities that will involve everyone, then allow people to connect as they wish—no hurt feelings allowed.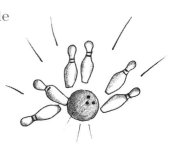

- Understand how hard it is for your husband when his kids leave.

- Although you can do a post-weekend wrap-up to discuss what you might do differently the next time, avoid blaming each other for anything that went wrong. Praise each other for what went right.

"When you are good friends first ... everything seems to take care of itself. ... Keep reminding yourself that your goal is to treat your partner with the same kindness, appreciation, and respect as you would your very best friend in the world."

—Richard Carlson, PhD, author

"**I** see how patient my husband is with my children—untangling fishing lines, tying ice skates, pumping up bicycle tires—and I am so grateful that the things I love about him as a partner translate to his stepparenting, and my kids benefit."

—Serena, mother of two, stepmother of one

311

Amarriage that can survive combining kids can survive anything.

312

You see wonderful qualities in him as a father that might have taken longer to uncover as just a spouse.

Conclusion

Silver Linings Found

My greatest blessing in writing this book was connecting with other stepmothers and swapping remarkably similar stories with women who understood. Like me, Beth expressed frustration with her stepchildren's mother, who tried so hard to prevent the kids from bonding with her. Like me, Grace admitted that she didn't always love her stepchildren as much as she thought she was supposed to. Like me, Janice revealed how her "Brady Bunch" expectations were immediately crushed when it was clear that she had stepchildren who weren't eager to embrace a new family dynamic. Like me, Viv admitted her shock at how dramatically a stepfamily differs from a first family.

Like all of the women I spoke with, I wanted to hear that our stepfamily challenges were common and could be overcome. I did hear that, and it relaxed and reassured me. I wish I'd written this book three years ago, when I was first embarking on my stepfamily adventure. There are few role models for stepmothers,  which means that we often have nowhere to turn for advice and comfort.

The simple act of thinking of a positive stepmom story to share for this book helped a number of moms I spoke with feel better about their family lives. One woman commented after our interview, "I was glad you asked me to share some of my happier stepmother stories with you. It's easy to get caught up in the struggles of parenting a blended family, but when I really thought back on the last few years, I realized how blessed we are as a family and I am as a mother. I have a loving relationship with each of my stepchildren, as well as my children. No relationship is perfect, but we appreciate and respect each other, we enjoy spending time together, and we have become integral parts of each other's lives. I'm grateful for what I have."

Being a stepmom is like panning for family gold. You'll sift through a lot of sand, but now and then, just when you're about to give up hope, you'll find some precious nuggets. And the longer you stay at it, the more likely you are to find gold every time you sift.

Other books by
Cynthia L. Copeland

Really Important Stuff My Kids
Have Taught Me

The Diaper Diaries
*The Real Poop on a New Mom's
First Year*

Fun on the Run!
324 Instant Family Activities